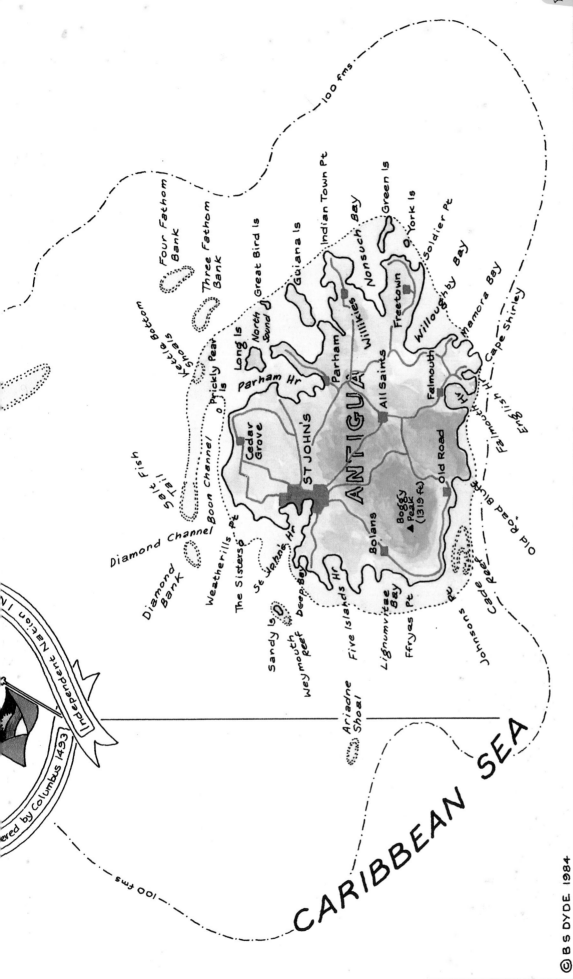

ANTIGUA

Boggy Peak (1319 ft)

CARIBBEAN SEA

S0-BDP-874

ANTIGUA & BARBUDA

A Little Bit of Paradise

HANSIB

Sunrise...each new day brings hope and inspiration

The English quickly recognised the value of English Harbour as a naval dockyard, being both defensible and a natural haven from hurricanes.

Sailing Week: Thousands of local people and visitors participate in Antigua's annual Sailing Week, which began in the 1960s and has grown into an international yachting event

Carnival is an explosion of colourful costumes, calypso rhythms, body language and a people's determination to enjoy life

First published in 1988 by Hansib Publishing Limited
Second revised edition published in 1994 by Hansib Publishing Limited
This third revised edition published in 1996
by Hansib Publishing (Caribbean) Limited
PO Box 2773, St John's, Antigua, WI

Colour origination by Graphic Ideas Studios, London
Printed in the United Kingdom by Bath Press Colourbooks, Glasgow

ISBN 1-870518-53-5

The publisher wishes to thank the following companies, who at an early stage, gave their support to the
publication of this book:
Ace Enterprises Limited; American International Bank; Antigua Management and Trust; Antours; Antigua Barbuda
Investment Bank Limited (Antigua Overseas Bank Limited, ABI Trust Limited); Antigua Commercial Bank; Antigua Public
Utilities Authority (APUA); Antigua Motors Limited; Barrymore Hotel; Curtain Bluff; Food City; Francis Trading Agency
Limited; Global Travel & Tours Limited; Hadeed Motors; Harney Motors; Hawksbill Beach Resort; Heritage Quay Hotel;
Joe Mikes; Joseph's Jolly Castle Hotel & Supermarket; Jolly Harbour; LIAT; The Linen Shop; Medical Benefits Scheme;
Runaway Beach Club; Shoul's Toys, Gifts & Housewares; State Insurance Corporation; Swiss American Bank; University of
Health Sciences, Antigua School of Medicine

THE NATIONAL COAT OF ARMS OF ANTIGUA AND BARBUDA

The **Pineapple** on top of the heraldic helmet represents the famous Antigua Black pineapple.

The **Red Hibiscus flowers** are symbolic of the many varieties of this plant found in abundance on the islands.

The **Shield with the Golden Sun** and **wavy blue and white bands** of the National Flag symbolises the sun, sea and beaches for which Antigua and Barbuda are renowned.

The **Old Sugar Mill** and the **stem of sugar cane** have historical roots and depict the cultivation of sugar cane for the production of sugar, which was Antigua's main industry.

The **Yucca plant** or "Spanish Bayonet", with its upright stem and showy edible flower cluster at its summit was the old emblem of Antigua.

The **deer** are symbolic of the wild-life that inhabited pre-colonial Antigua and Barbuda.

The **scroll** bears the Motto of the Nation "Each Endeavouring, All Achieving."

THE DESIGNER OF THE COAT OF ARMS

The National Coat of Arms was designed by Gordon Christopher with some modification by the Statehood Celebrations Committee, 1966. Mr Christopher was born in Antigua and emigrated to Canada in 1967. He gained, in 1971, a diploma in Applied Art at the Alberta College of Art and, at the University of Calgary, graduated with a Bachelor of Fine Arts Degree in 1974. Since then, he has been an active painter, printmaker, graphic designer and instructor in art. His work has been exhibited both nationally and internationally and is included in private and public collections in Canada and the United States. He is a member of the Alberta Society of Artists.

THE MOTTO OF THE NATION

The Motto of the Nation: "Each Endeavouring, All Achieving" was composed by Mr James H Carrott MBE in 1967. Mr Carrott was then Permanent Secretary in the Ministry of Trade, Production and Labour. According to Mr Carrott: "The concept was to provide inspiration to each Antiguan and Barbudan to recognise that the development of the whole country would be a benefit to all, but that development required the effort of each individual."

NATIONAL ANTHEM OF ANTIGUA AND BARBUDA

Words by Novelle H Richards, Music by Walter P Chambers, Arrangement by H A Kenney

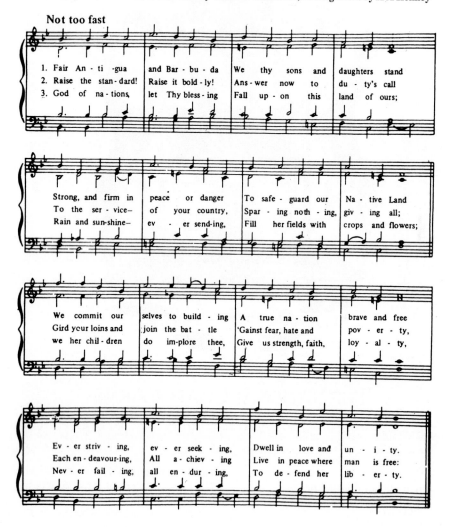

ABOUT THE MAIN CONTRIBUTORS

RON SANDERS

Ron Sanders has written widely on the Caribbean. His work has been published in academic journals such as *Caribbean Affairs* and *Round Table* - the Commonwealth Journal of International Affairs (Institute of Commonwealth Studies, London University). He has also contributed chapters to several books including *Europe and the Caribbean* (Macmillan, 1991), *Democracy in the Caribbean* (John Hopkins University Press, 1993). He has written editorial opinions for the Caribbean press through the Caribbean News Agency and in London for the *Caribbean Times*.

He is a former broadcaster having been President of the Caribbean Broadcasting Union, a Director of the Caribbean News Agency and a presenter and interviewer on the BBC's World Service. He presented the BBC's flagship current affairs programme *"24 Hours"* and *"Development"*. He was also a regular contributor to *"Commentary after the News"*.

Sanders served as Antigua and Barbuda's Deputy Permanent Representative to the UN (1981-82), Ambassador to UNESCO (1983-87) and High Commissioner to the United Kingdom (1984-87). In 1983, he was elected for a two year term to the Council of the International Programme for the Development of Communication at UNESCO, and in 1985, he was elected to the Governing Board of UNESCO for a two-year term.

Between 1987 and 1989, he was a Visiting Fellow at Oxford University before working as an International Relations Consultant to several multinational corporations on whose boards of directors he served.

At the time of this publication he was on a second tour of duty as Antigua and Barbuda's High Commissioner to London and Ambassador to Germany and France.

ALLAN AFLAK

Allan Aflak is a young Antiguan photographer and businessman who has been extensively involved in both editions of *A Little Bit of Paradise*. He has provided most of the photographs for both books and is now the exclusive distributor in Antigua. His other businesses include 'Island Photo', a one-hour photo lab and camera store, and 'The Photo Shop', which is a supplier of photography and related supplies to many of the hotels and tourist shops around the island.

Allan is a graduate of the St Joseph's Academy in Antigua and has a Bachelor of Arts with a major in Psychology from St Mary's University in Halifax, Nova Scotia. His photographs have been published extensively throughout the Caribbean, North America and Europe.

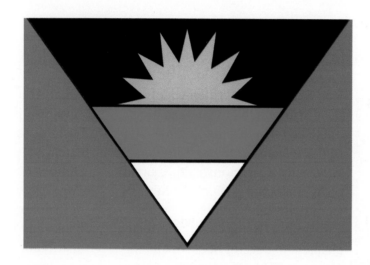

The National Flag of Antigua and Barbuda

The Golden Sun - symbolises the dawn of a new era.
Red - symbolises the dynamism of the people
Blue - symbolises hope.
Black - symbolises the soil and our African heritage.
Gold, Blue and White together represent Antigua's tourist
attractions - sun, sea and sand.
The "V" depicted in the design by the Black, Blue and White
bands is the symbol of victory.

Designer of the Flag

**The Flag of Antigua and Barbuda was
designed in 1967 when the country became a
State in Association with Britain. Its designer,
Reginald Samuel (left), is an Antiguan artist,
sculptor, painter and art teacher. His design
was selected from among 600 entries.**

CONTENTS

Above: Carlisle Bay

Front Cover: (Main picture) Runaway Bay. (Inset clockwise from top left) Antigua Sailing Week; Runaway Beach; Betty's Hope; Frigate Bird Sanctuary, Barbuda; Carnival Antigua; English Harbour.

Back cover: (Clockwise from top left) Underwater Antigua; sunrise at Cades Bay; Blue Waters Resort; cannon at Fort James; a morning swim at Marina Bay; Cricket - the number-one sport; St John's Cathedral.

Additional photographs, maps and other references courtesy of: Ronald Sanders; Antigua and Barbuda Adventure Tourist Guide; Time Out Antigua; Allsport, London; Jolly Harbour Complex; Blue Waters Hotel; Brian Dyde, Antigua and Barbuda Heart of the Caribbean; What's Happening; Kenneth Gibbs; Henry Christian.

FOREWORD

elcome to the third edition of 'Antigua and Barbuda - A Little Bit of Paradise'.

When Prime Minister Lester Bird (then Deputy Prime Minister and Minister of Foreign Affairs) commissioned the first edition back in 1988, we threw ourselves with enthusiasm into producing the pioneer volume.

Like every first venture, its form and shape evolved as the work progressed.

However, it was a great success and the first edition was completely sold out with demands for more.

Of course, the production of a second, and now a third edition, besides chronicling fresh developments, is a chance to improve and consolidate the contents. This is evident from the results.

Among the new features to be found in this edition, is a German-language synopsis, reflecting both the growing interest of Europe's leading economy in what the Caribbean has to offer as a tourist destination.

Antigua and Barbuda is a country on the move - and on the way up. It is, in many ways, a model of development. It is a respected player on the world stage, a fact highlighted at the time of writing by the just-concluded, and highly successful, official visit to the United Kingdom by Prime Minister Lester Bird.

In contrast to many other countries undergoing political reforms, Antigua and Barbuda has always been deeply attached to the concept and values of parliamentary democracy.

After the most recent general election in 1994, the governing Antigua Labour Party (ALP) holds 11 seats, the United Progressive Party (UPP) opposition has five seats and the representative from Barbuda has the remaining seat.

The biggest political change - although one that also symbolises continuity - has been the assumption of the Prime Ministership by Lester Bird.

When Lester Bird assumed the reins of the country's governance, he undertook to

LESTER BIRD, Prime Minister of Antigua & Barbuda

stabilise its fiscal situation and to lay the foundation for future growth by cutting waste and spending more on health, education and physical infrastructure. His government has started that process, even though it has received criticism from some of those who were beneficiaries of government programmes that have been drastically reduced.

To an overwhelming degree, Antigua and Barbuda depends on the tourist industry for its economic well-being.

Yet it is from this foundation that Antigua and Barbuda has moved to maintain and develop the quality of its people's lives, steadily increasing the resources made available for health, education and all the various services essential to the construction of a modern and civilised country.

All this was put to the test in September 1995 when Hurricane Luis struck the country. But Antigua and Barbuda rose to the challenge, and anyone visiting the country today, would be hard pressed to recognise that Hurricane Luis had ever struck. A remarkable rehabilitation drive succeeded in putting right all the

damage - in many respects the country is now better equipped and more welcoming than before. Telephone, electricity and water services are amongst the best in the Caribbean. The government's programme to rehabilitate all Antigua's major roads is just one in a series of efforts to dramatically upgrade the national infrastructure.

Antigua and Barbuda is now gearing itself up to face the challenges of the twenty-first century.

We hope that this present volume will serve as a record of the achievements made to date and as a pointer towards an even brighter future.

Arif Ali
June 1996

PARADISE PRESENTED

Welcome to paradise - pearls of natural beauty set in the jewel of the blue Caribbean sea! Before we unfold the drama of the settlement, colonisation and evolution of these islands, we should survey the scene of the activity.

The territory of Antigua and Barbuda actually consists of three main islands Antigua, Barbuda and Redonda although there are several small dependent islands around Antigua such as Guiana Island, Bird Island and Long Island. Antigua is 108 square miles (280 sq km), Barbuda is 62 sq miles (160 sq km) and Redonda is 0.6 sq miles (1.6 sq km).

Redonda is uninhabited and there are approximately 63,000 people on Antigua and 1,252 on Barbuda. The last population census was done in 1991. When the previous census was conducted in the 1980's, Antigua's population was 78,000 and Barbuda's 1,500. This decline in population is due to the emigration of native Antiguans and Barbudans. Since the 1930s, many families have ensured that at least one child is born in the United States of America, allowing for other family members to emigrate there - pursuing a different kind of paradise.

Ninety-one percent of the people of Antigua and Barbuda are of African descent. Their forefathers were brought as slaves in the 17th and 18th centuries from the West Coast of Africa. The rest of the population is made up of Lebanese and Syrians who came as traders at the beginning of this century; the descendants of Portuguese - 2,500 of whom came as labourers from Madeira between 1847, when a famine plagued that island, and 1852; Americans, Canadians and Europeans who settled during this century and West Indians mainly from Dominica, Montserrat, St Kitts and Guyana. Recently, there has been a small influx of Chinese from the Peoples Republic of China who entered the country as workers in the small garment industry. Some have since opened modest Chinese restaurants.

The political structure of the country is firmly rooted in parliamentary democracy patterned on the system in Britain. There are several political parties which contest elections at least every five years when Antiguans and Barbudans of eighteen and over can vote to choose a government. The country is divided into 17 constituencies and parties contesting the elections nominate one candidate for election in each constituency. A general election is won by the party whose candidates are elected in nine or more constituencies. The victorious party then forms a government consisting of a Prime Minister and several Ministers.

The State system comprises the government,

Parliament Building

The new Governor-General, Sir James B. Carlisle being welcomed in Parliament by Prime Minister V. C. Bird

The Museum

Governor-General, Sir James Beethoven Carlisle, GCMG, on a tour of inspection

parliament, the judiciary and the Head of State.

Antigua and Barbuda's Head of State is Queen Elizabeth II who is also Head of State in Britain and several other Commonwealth countries. The Queen is represented in Antigua and Barbuda by a Governor-General selected by the Government. The role of the Head of State is largely ceremonial although the Constitution of the country vests certain limited powers in the office.

Parliament has two chambers - an assembly of representatives of parties or individuals who are elected by the majority votes in the constituencies,

and a Senate whose members are appointed by the Governor-General, the Prime Minister and the leader of the opposition in parliament. Parliament makes the laws of the country.

The Judiciary is entirely independent of the government. Both judges and appeal court judges are appointed by the consensus of seven governments in the Eastern Caribbean. This makes it difficult for individual governments to attempt to influence the Court against its own judgement of the law.

This is the scene of paradise on which our story begins...

Morning has Broken

The sun, like a huge, ripe orange, rises slowly from behind the Caribbean sea. Streaks of light - some yellow, some red, yet others brightly white - strike out across the water, dancing on the peaks of gentle, little waves as they meander towards a shore still cast in night's receding shadow, but already exposing beaches of white and golden sands. It is daybreak in Antigua and Barbuda... and everyday is summer.

As the sun ascends - boldly now, for, like the day, it too is fully awake - its golden glow begins to disappear, yielding to a stunning brightness which hurls itself across the sea and onto the land. The atmosphere is still cool, for even though the sun has begun to proclaim its dominion over the earth, its heat is still young and unable to penetrate the cool, North East Trade Winds which blow steadily across the sea.

In an age old tradition, tiny fishing boats oscillate on the sea, making their way back to the shore, laden with fish for the morning's market. The fishermen set sail during the night knowing that daybreak would lure fish to the sea's surface in ritual welcome to the radiance of a newborn sun before its heat forced them to seek cooler waters near the ocean floor. The rhythmic chug of the fishing boats' small, outboard engines mixes with the louder roar of bigger engines on jet-skis, motor boats and yachts as those who cater for visitors begin to prepare their equipment for the day's coterie of people anxious to make the most of a Caribbean holiday.

Slowly now, people begin to appear: first, young natives of Antigua and Barbuda - their bodies bristling with health, their muscles well developed - jogging along the beach and occasionally diving into the water to be refreshed by its invigorating sting. Visitors too come in this early morning light and, with a sense of longing at last fulfilled, immerse themselves into the sea, stretching out on their backs, relaxing their muscles, letting tensions dissipate, their faces raised to catch the tingling touch of the sun's glorious rays.

Birds too are part of the morning's activity. There are 140 species on Antigua and Barbuda, 90 of which are seen regularly. Some are hunters - such as the Brown Pelicans skimming along the sea, suddenly plunging into the water only to rise again abruptly, their morning meal caught in their beaks. Others flit from tree to tree calling out in song and adding to the ambience of nature in all its perfection. The Bananaquit and the Lesser Antillean Bullfinch, black or grey with a reddish breast are the most common.

As the sun gains in ascendancy, bathing the land

ABOVE: Early morning jogger on Dickenson Bay
RIGHT: Local bathers on Runaway Bay

in light, colours come alive - leaves are now vivid green, flowers - the exotic bougainvillaea, the hibiscus and the oleander - are red, yellow, white and even purple.

Coconut trees and other palms, that have stood majestically on the shores of these islands for decades, climb upwards toward the clear blue sky dotted only here and there with soft, white clouds. Occasionally either a very old or a very young palm, responding to pressure from the wind, arches downwards - but even this curve has a certain grace, an attractiveness that

speaks not of submission to an unwelcome force, but of surrender to the allure of nature.

The shores - 365 beaches and coves - are the beginnings of "a little bit of paradise", the same paradise that Christopher Columbus encountered on 11 November 1493 when on his second journey to what he called the 'new world', he saw the islands and, without setting foot on them, named one 'Barbuda', and the other 'Antigua' after the miracle working Virgin, Santa Maria la Antigua, in Seville Cathedral, Spain.

Local fishing boats in St John's Harbour

Sports fishing boat heading out to sea

The Wizard catamaran getting ready to leave for a day trip

As the sun gains ascendancy, bathing the land in light, flowers and plants come alive

ABOVE: A pelican diving in St John's Harbour
LEFT: A brown Pelican

There are 140 species of birds on Antigua and Barbuda

Coconut trees provide a little shade for the tennis courts at Curtain Bluff

MORNING BEFORE YESTERDAY

M an inhabited these islands before Christ was born. According to a group of experts:

"It may have been in the neighbourhood of ten thousand years before Christ that the first Amerindians, who we now call Paleo-Indians, navigated by primitive canoe to thread their way between Antigua and Barbuda's barrier reef to land on her white sandy beaches. Sea levels were then at least 275 feet lower than they are today so that Antigua and Barbuda were linked together."

It has been established that people of the Meso-Indian age lived on Antigua as far back as 1775 BC at Jolly Beach. They were called the 'Siboney' (stone people). While around 500 BC, nomadic wanderers lived and fished at North Sound, there were no settlements on the island until 35 AD when some Amerindians of the Arawak tribe moved from their home in Venezuela and settled near Indian Creek establishing fishing villages, some agriculture and pottery. Around 1200 AD another tribe of Amerindians, the Caribs, also came up the chain of islands from South America. They established settlements in Dominica and St Kitts from where they attacked the Arawaks on Antigua taking their women and children as slaves and murdering the men. They called Antigua, 'Waladli', Barbuda, 'Wa'omoni' and Redonda, 'Ocanamanru'.

Antigua: The foundation of Antigua is a large mass of volcanic rock, occupying 40-45% of the 108 square miles (280 sq km) of the island, the rest of it is formed of sedimentary rocks, mainly limestone.

Antigua can be divided into three principal regions:
    -a high region consisting of precipitous hills of volcanic formation, many over 1,000 feet high. The highest point is Boggy Peak at just over 1,300 feet;
    -a rolling lowland (knows as the central plain) running from St John's, the Capital City, in the north-west to the spectacular Willoughby Bay in the south-east, and occupying about 20 square miles of the island; and
    - a limestone area between the hills and the plain.

Antigua's shape has been described as akin to an ink blot. Its coastline - over 90 miles long - is jagged creating hundreds of coves and bays, many with fine white sand. There are also extensive coral reefs which not only maintain magnificent marine life, but also protect the coast from erosion and provide calm waters in the bays.

Boggy Peak - the highest point in Antigua - houses a modern communication system which keeps the nation in touch worldwide

Pillars of Hercules

Aerial view of Willoughby Bay and its outlying coral reef

Barbuda's east coastline is protected by coral reef and is difficult for shipping but excellent for scuba diving

The island gets very little rainfall, an average of 45 inches a year. Droughts are common place and sometimes there is no rainfall for years. This absence of rain is due in great measure to the policy of the colonial sugar planters who wantonly cut down trees to plant sugar cane.

Previously, the island was lush and thickly wooded. It had evergreen forests of red and white cedar and whitewood. In the forests lived colourful birds including the parrot. After almost a century of forest destruction, a Governor of the Island, Thomas Shirley, was forced to record in 1781:

> "By this injudicious step, the fruits of the earth are deprived of those periodical supplies of moisture from rain... four or five years of dry weather will occur scorching with heat the whole island."

Barbuda: Barbuda is mostly a flat plain except for a small area called The Highlands which rises to a maximum of 128 feet. The entire island is a limestone formation. It gets less rainfall than Antigua and has no streams or lakes, However, its beach at Coco Point is regarded by many seasoned travellers as the most beautiful in the Caribbean. Almost the whole coastline of Barbuda is edged with coral reefs which simultaneously makes it dangerous for shipping and majestic for scuba divers.

Redonda: The majority of Antiguans and Barbudans have never seen Redonda which has always been an 'isolated, precipitous and forbidding rocky island'. It is one mile long and less than half a mile wide rising to 1,000 feet with steep cliffs on all sides. On 10 November 1493, the day before he sailed past Antigua, Columbus by-passed the rock and, in the process, named it Santa Maria la Redonda. Over the years it has been used in a variety of transient ways, including growing cassava for seafarers on the saddle on the top of the rock, issuing postage stamps and mining phosphates from bird guano. However, it is only as a haven for birds that it remains useful.

YESTERDAY MORN'

Antigua was first settled by Europeans in an area now called **Old Road.** The settlers were English and, led by Captain Edward Warner, came from England's principal West Indian colony, St Kitts. Apart from a brief period in 1666 when it was captured by the French, Antigua remained British until its independence on 1 November, 1981. Today the country continues to be a Monarchical State sharing Queen Elizabeth 11 as its Head of State with Britain and several other Commonwealth countries. Barbuda used to be a separate British possession until 1 August, 1860 when it was formally annexed to Antigua.

The man directly responsible for the link between Antigua and Barbuda was Sir Christopher Codrington who came to Antigua from Barbados in 1674 and established the first large sugar estate, which he named **Betty's Hope**, after his daughter. Located on the south side of the main road to **Long Bay**, the ruins of the estate house and a working wind mill today provide an insight into the activity on this plantation three centuries ago.

Sugar production dominated Antigua until the 1970s, utilising most of the land and leaving a legacy of grave economic problems. Previously, tobacco was the main crop produced by the settlers on Antigua.

On 6 January 1685, Codrington was also granted a lease of Barbuda from the British Crown as an annexe to his estates on Antigua. The annual fee required of him for the lease was 'one fat sheep if asked'. From Barbuda, the Codringtons supplied their Antigua holdings with timber, ground provisions, fish, livestock and draught animals for more than 200 years.

It has been suggested that Barbuda was a 'stud farm' on which the Codringtons bred 'quality slaves'. Even Barbudans themselves tended to believe this, hence the Barbuda Brotherhood Social Club of New York is reported as asserting in a 1977 publication that "Barbuda was used as the experimental breeding ground for slaves, thus producing some of the strongest people in the West Indies." However, scholarly research of this claim debunks it completely. Having studied the period and the documents related to it, two eminent scholars, David Lowenthal and Colin G Clarke record:

> "There never was a deliberate program
> of slave breeding in Barbuda, nor did
> the Codringtons ever contemplate this
> as a possibility. At the very most they
> envisaged Barbuda as a "nursery" to
> which slave children might be brought

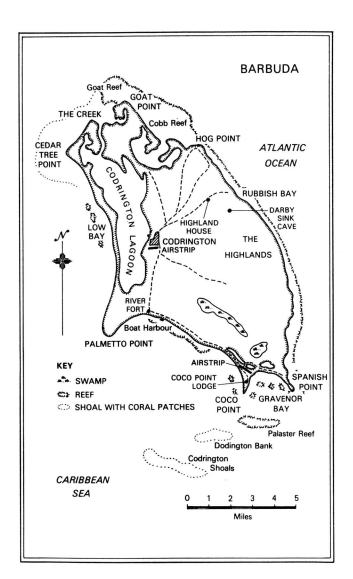

BARBUDA

Goat Reef
GOAT POINT
THE CREEK
Cobb Reef
HOG POINT
CEDAR TREE POINT

ATLANTIC OCEAN

CODRINGTON LAGOON

RUBBISH BAY

DARBY SINK CAVE

HIGHLAND HOUSE
CODRINGTON AIRSTRIP

LOW BAY

THE HIGHLANDS

RIVER FORT
Boat Harbour
PALMETTO POINT

AIRSTRIP
COCO POINT LODGE
COCO POINT
GRAVENOR BAY
SPANISH POINT

Palaster Reef
Dodington Bank
Codrington Shoals

CARIBBEAN SEA

KEY
🔺 SWAMP
🪸 REEF
〰️ SHOAL WITH CORAL PATCHES

0 1 2 3 4 5
Miles

ABOVE: There are no tarmac roads on Barbuda

LEFT: Barbuda is about 62 miles square including the Codrington Lagoon. Two thirds of the island consists of a flat plain only a few feet above sea level. The remaining third, known as The Highlands, is a flat table land rising to a maximum of 128 feet above sea level

BELOW: Antigua is 1200 miles south of Miami, Florida and 3540 miles from London, England

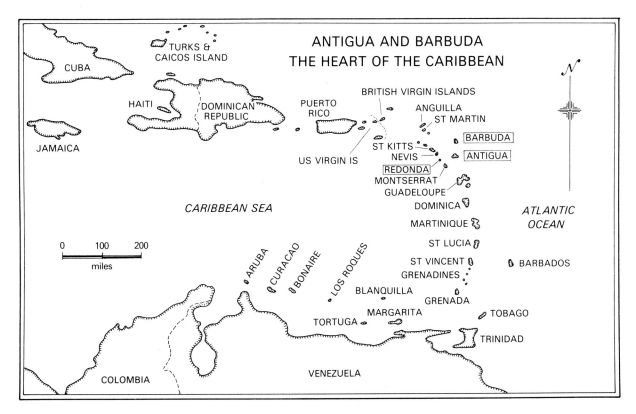

ANTIGUA AND BARBUDA
THE HEART OF THE CARIBBEAN

TURKS & CAICOS ISLAND

CUBA

HAITI

DOMINICAN REPUBLIC

PUERTO RICO

BRITISH VIRGIN ISLANDS

ANGUILLA
ST MARTIN

JAMAICA

US VIRGIN IS

ST KITTS
NEVIS
REDONDA
MONTSERRAT
GUADELOUPE

BARBUDA
ANTIGUA

CARIBBEAN SEA

DOMINICA

MARTINIQUE

ATLANTIC OCEAN

0 100 200
miles

ARUBA
CURACAO
BONAIRE
LOS ROQUES

ST LUCIA

ST VINCENT
GRENADINES

BARBADOS

BLANQUILLA
GRENADA

MARGARITA
TOBAGO

TORTUGA

TRINIDAD

COLOMBIA

VENEZUELA

Betty's Hope sugar plantation in Antigua was established in 1674 to introduce large scale sugar production

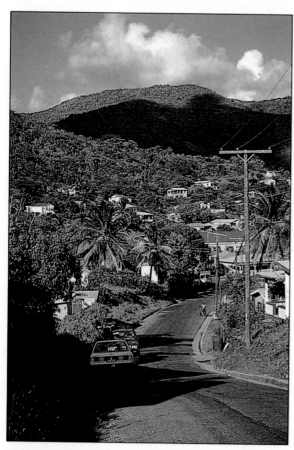

From 1685 to 1870, the Codringtons also leased Barbuda for "one fat sheep per year" thus forging the link between the two islands.

Betty's Hope

Old Road village

Welcome to Betty's Hope

Fig Tree Drive, from the town of Liberta to Old Road at Carlisle Bay is lined with lush vegetation. The road twists and climbs through Antigua's most scenic hillsides and the island's rainforest. There is a rainforest guide at the Fig Tree Drive Culture Shoppe

Slave Market - by 1678 half of Antigua's population consisted of African slaves

to be fed and cared for, and later taken off to work on the Antigua estates, but not even this proposal was realized."

Apart from providing food and livestock to their Antigua plantations, Barbuda's principal benefit to the Codringtons was a base from which to salvage ships which ran aground or wrecked on the reefs off Barbuda. The profits from the salvage operations went to the Codringtons who owned the men, boats and all the "equipment available for salvage operations."

Codrington's success with sugar encouraged other planters and soon there was a proliferation of sugar estates across Antigua. By 1705 most of the island was planted and 170 mills were erected for crushing cane. The windmills replaced the earlier oxen-driven mills and output of sugar per factory more than doubled. Many of these mills can still be seen today around the island.

Accompanying the spread of sugar estates was the almost complete annihilation of vegetation. As Gregson Davis put it in 'Antigua Black', 'the evergreen woodland was levelled in a manner as thorough as it was irreversible and short-sighted'. Hence apart from the lush **Fig Tree Drive**, there is a lamentable absence of forests and woods in Antigua today. But the defacing of the natural beauty of the island was not the only consequence of the wanton destruction of vegetation: as noted earlier, drought was the principal result of an absence of trees to attract rainfall. The government has sought to tackle this problem by creating **Potswork Dam**, a huge man-made lake in the centre of Antigua, and installing desalinisation plants to convert sea water for domestic and industrial use.

By 1678, half the island's population consisted of slaves brought from the West Coast of Africa to cultivate sugar. The harrowing and inhuman system of slavery is well known. The lot of the slaves in Antigua was no different from their counterparts in the Caribbean and North and South America - the Antigua slaves were whipped and worked from sun up to sun down; resistance was met with foul punishments including dismembering of the body.

The desalination plant is vital to Antigua because of low rainfall

An aerial view of man-made Potswork Dam in the centre of Antigua

Barbuda: an east coast look-out cottage built beside a rock - possibly as camouflage from passing ships. It was used to report on shipwrecks

The caves under Barbuda's Highlands are full of surprises and offer clues to the island's formation

Game and livestock have been the main-stay of the Barbudan economy and with limited rainfall it is essential to use drinking water wisely. This watering trough is about forty feet long and is attached to a deep natural well. It is used by wild and domestic animals

Beaches on Barbuda are incredibly stunning and remarkably short of people

Naturally, many rebelled and only musket and shot compelled them to remain captive.

Some particular events relevant to Antigua are worth recalling here. In 1789 and repeatedly until 1816, the Codrington family, who had taken up residence in Gloucester, England, wrote letters to the managers of their estates on Antigua decrying William Wilberforce - who pioneered in the British Parliament first, the Act to end the slave trade and then the abolition of slavery itself. Undoubtedly, they would also have used every influence in England to thwart the efforts of Wilberforce and the abolitionists.

Meanwhile, conditions on Antigua for the slave remained appalling resulting in seven revolts and six major conspiracies between 1640 and 1713. Running away was a frequent means of escape from the brutal conditions on Antiguan plantations. Runaways formed a community on Antigua's highest hill, Boggy Peak, and in 1684, the Government posted bounties of £2.10s for the capture of live slaves and £1 for dead ones. In 1688, the militia stormed the camp and burned the leaders to ashes.

After the slave trade was abolished in 1807, rebellions became more frequent. This explodes the myth, perpetrated by the apologists for slavery, that slaves were somehow content with their condition. In reality, early slaves - from various tribes and speaking different languages - could not communicate among themselves. Thus, they were unable to discuss their plight, let alone plot an insurrection. This policy of importing slaves from diverse tribes continued for years, the first coming from modern Liberia, Ghana, Togo, Dahomey and Western Nigeria. It is the process of 'creolisation' that produced the conditions for slave resistance. After 1807, the majority of slaves, having been born in the Caribbean, were able to communicate with each other and were not constrained by the tribal prejudices of their forebears.

In 1831, just three years before slavery was abolished, there was an insurrectionary movement on Antigua in protest at the prohibition of the Negro Sunday Market at which slaves sold their private production. The insurrection was so widespread that the Governor of Barbados had to send reinforcements to help the militia in Antigua put down the rebellion.

By comparison, the slaves on Barbuda had a relatively easy life if it is possible to discount the reprehensible system of slavery itself. As West Indian Historian Douglas Hall notes:

ABOVE: Spiney Hill Perk, proudly flies the Union Jack flag on the corn and sweet potato farm

RIGHT: At Codrington pier, visitors can get a boat to the Frigate Sanctuary. Pictured is George Burton, civic councillor and tour operator, booking a tour with Tyrone Beaser, boat handler and Frigate Sanctuary guide

"For the slaves, Barbuda was a relatively happy place. They were engaged, largely in pastoral and hunting occupations or as skilled workers in wood and leather. Many became expert sailors and fishermen. Above all, they were not subject to the tyranny of the cane fields."

Unlike the slaves on Antigua, those on Barbuda "enjoyed an abundance of provisions from their large garden plots, from hunting game in the forests, and from fishing". They had at most three white overseers and lived virtually on their own. Significantly, the Barbudan slaves deeply resented being transferred to Antigua. The first such recorded transfer was in 1779. Even though they were slaves, the Barbudans "adamantly rejected emigration to the Antigua plantations". In 1831, Codrington's manager in Antigua wrote to him explaining that many of the Barbudans died shortly after transfer to the Antigua estates, and he added:

"On Barbuda, they ramble through the woods all hours of the night, taking any thing that comes in their way, either deer, sheep or cattle, as required... They are used to live on fresh meat which

they do not get here... When here they cannot stop in their houses at night, but are foraging at all hours, and the air is very different to Barbuda, being damp and chilly, they often take violent colds and fall into dropsy."

23,350 slaves on Antigua were emancipated on 1 August 1834 along with those in The Bahamas and Bermuda. In all of the other British colonies in the Caribbean, there was a four year transition period, called apprenticeship, before full freedom was granted.

But, the immediate emancipation of the slaves was no act of benevolence as will become apparent later in this text.

The freed slaves in Antigua woke up on **Emancipation Day** as landless wage earners paid the princely sum of one shilling per day. They had nothing except a notional freedom, for they owned nothing and had no choice but to continue working on the sugar plantations of their former masters. And, therein lies the real reason for the full emancipation of the Antiguan slaves without apprenticeship.

The sugar planters received £415,713 from the British Treasury as compensation for the slaves they

Aerial view of Codrington, Barbuda

lost. In addition they obtained a large and captive workforce. Since the slaves had no means of earning a living other than by working on the sugar estates, the plantation owners freed them, paid them a derisory wage and evaded the burden of feeding, clothing and housing them. One planter, at a meeting of proprietors prior to the decision on whether or not to institute a period of apprenticeship, actually proposed full emancipation because it was more profitable. The planter

> "produced statements to show that
> under a free system he would have to
> pay wages to one third only of the
> negroes whom he should be required to
> support as apprentices; and that he
> could work his estates equally well by
> free labour, at a less expense."

Despite their gain, the planters still took a number of steps to restrict the former slaves on Antigua. First, they passed the Contract Act under which the former slaves were made to sign contracts of employment imposing penalties for breaches. These penalties ranged from loss of wages for minor infractions to imprisonment for what they determined to be major infringements such as missing two days work in a fortnight. Then, they reduced the amount

of land on their estates available for workers to cultivate food crops. This made the workers increasingly dependent on their wages to purchase food and therefore tied them more firmly to the sugar estates.

The freedom of the liberated slaves was further constrained in October 1836 with the passage of the Police Act by which the planters prohibited country people from bringing their goods to market without a pass from the manager of the estate on which they resided. Without such a pass, the police were empowered to seize their property. Two Englishmen, who were in Antigua at the time the Act was passed, recorded the following account given to them by a former slave of the importance of selling their produce:

> "The wage of one shilling per day was
> not enough to maintain them. He had a
> wife and six children, and an old
> mother to support; of whom, two of the
> children only were able to earn any
> thing. They could not manage without
> "minding" their little stock. He said
> that if a labourer was five minutes after
> time in the morning, the manager
> stopped his pay for the day. He

Peaceful and green countryside in the centre of Antigua

Coco Point is deservedly called 'the finest beach in the Caribbean'

ABOVE: Bougainvillea is the most common and colourful vine in the Caribbean. The main colours range from red through to purple to magenta

LEFT: A ten feet high cactus growing in Barbuda's Highlands

complained also that he had just received thirty days notice to quit because he refused to allow one of his children whom he wished to put to trade, to go to the field, although he promised that all his other children should be brought up to estate labour."

Many of the freed slaves emigrated to Guyana and Trinidad where better wages were being paid for labour on larger and less populated estates. Recognising the haemorrhaging of their exploited labour, the planters on Antigua passed an Act for "preventing clandestine deportation of labourers, artificers, handicraftsmen and domestic servants from the island".

But as the oppressive conditions on the sugar estates continued, so too did migration. This created a shortage of labour in the early 1890s. To meet their need for labour, the planters imported 500 Chinese but, according to one writer, "owing to the absence of contracts, the immigration was not so successful as it might have been, but it relieved the pressure at the time."

It is a tribute to the tenacity and industry of the former slaves that in the four years following emancipation, despite the brutality from which they

had recently emerged and the deprivation into which they were delivered, they moved from being landless wage earners to possessors of 1,037 houses in 27 villages. They bought plots of land on hire purchase and met their payments faithfully. After working a full day on the sugar plantations, they went home to cultivate their front and back gardens with plantains, yams, bananas and pineapples. They even found time to grow flowers. Their carefully laid out plots with their pretty gardens can still be seen today in villages such as Liberta, the first of the free villages to be created.

In the meantime, Barbuda was so little remembered in Britain that the draftsmen of the Bill for the Abolition of Slavery had omitted it in the document. Codrington continued to maintain the former slaves on Barbuda, then numbering about 500, but on 2 April 1860, he wrote a letter addressed to all of them suggesting that they go to work on his estates in Antigua because there was nothing for them to do on Barbuda. They refused.

Paradoxically, the conditions of relative ease which existed for the Barbudans during slavery changed after the Abolition Act was passed.

Sir Bethel Codrington completely freed his slaves on Barbuda in 1834, even though Barbuda had not

Visitors to Antigua & Barbuda cannot fail to be impressed by the richness of flora

been listed in the Abolition Law. Having done so, he was faced with the problem that 500 people, now living on his property, were dependent on him but did not belong to him.

Codrington's agent therefore drew up an Agreement in 1835 to deal with this new situation. In summary, the Agreement stated that:

> -all workers' provision-grounds were to be sited within a short radius around the village;
> -the Barbudans would have the right 'to set Pots and Trammels to catch fish in the Lagoon' - but in no other manner and in no other place without express permission;
> - the Barbudans would be allowed to gather cashews and cashew-nuts only from trees growing on their provision-grounds, and even there the proprietor might earmark certain trees for his own use;
> - Barbudans could catch crabs at Sand Bank or King's Hall - but nowhere else without express permission;
> -labourers were forbidden to trespass or commit injury upon any land, cultivated

or not, 'from which they have been hitherto prohibited', under such penalty as the Governor might deem expedient;- freedom of movement beyond Barbuda was also limited. Any three labourers, at any one time, would be allowed to go to Antigua in one of the Codringtons' vessels in order to sell and buy goods, but they should not stay longer than three days and this privilege could be enjoyed only once in every four months.

This arrangement - while it placed restrictions on the Barbudans that they had not experienced under slavery - did not turn out to be advantageous for the Codringtons. The cost of maintaining the Barbudans proved to be greater than the earnings the island produced. By deed poll executed on 13 July 1870, the Codringtons surrendered their lease 35 years before it was due to expire in 1905. Thus ended the long association between the Codringtons and Barbuda.

In the meantime, the Antigua legislature had been given responsibility for Barbuda in 1858, an obligation they accepted only on the proviso that it would cost them no money. On 1 August, 1860, by

an Order-in-Council signed by the British Monarch at the Isle of Wight, Barbuda was annexed to Antigua. Neither the Antigua legislature nor the freed slaves on Barbuda were happy with this development - the former because they felt it would be a burden on their treasury and the latter because they disliked Antigua which, over the years had become a place of punishment in their minds since it was there that the unruly among them were sentenced, and many had died.

The Antiguan authorities tried to free themselves of spending money on Barbuda by leasing the island to new tenants. However, each lease ended in disaster and, finally, in November 1898, Barbuda was once again re-possessed by the Governor of the Leeward Islands and the Antiguan Legislature at last agreed to make financial provision for the island.

However, despite the new travail which the Barbudans experienced with lease-owners of the island, their antagonism toward Antigua did not decline. Indeed, Barbudan hostility to Antigua continued for another hundred years, and was evident when the Government of Antigua and Barbuda sought the country's independence from Britain.

There are several varieties of mangoes in Antigua

BITTER SUGAR

The fortunes of Britain in the 17th and 18th century may have been made on the sweetness of sugar, but colonial sugar policy in Antigua left the island a bitter legacy.

For over 200 years until the early 1950's, Antigua was deliberately made a monoculture economy - sugar. No attempt was made to introduce any other economic activity and, therefore, the country's fortune was inextricably tied to sugar for good or ill. Such skills as were developed among the people related entirely to the sugar estates. After the 1900's by which time the country's population had grown and prices for cane sugar had dropped, the shortsightedness of this "one crop economy" became evident. But, it had to confront the colonial power, unyielding and ugly, before any quarter was given to the introduction of other agricultural activity. After 1900, corn and cotton cultivation was allowed but sugar still reigned supreme.

Prior to 1834, the sugar plantations were organised on the basis of slave labour so, obviously, there was no question of benefits accruing to the workers. There was little change after slavery was abolished. The workers had no alternative but to return to the plantations to be paid atrociously low wages since all the land was owned by the sugar barons. The estate owners also refused to rent or lease land to the workers for fear that the labour force would be depleted. This unannounced policy continued until the early 1900's. Therefore, labour and land were completely tied up by the sugar barons and no cultivation of food crops was possible.

The estate owners insisted on the importation of food supplies. By this means, they made the workers captive to wages from the sugar estates in order to pay for imported food. Since sugar continued to occupy most of the arable land until 1972. Antigua's food import bill rose astronomically and by 1980 it represented over 25 per cent of the country's total imports in terms of cost.

Significantly, in the latter years of sugar cultivation in Antigua though it was the country's main export, it could not pay for the island's imports so that the balance of trade deficit rose from 0.9 per cent in 1950 to 45.4 per cent in 1970.

Aside from a legacy of very little food production in Antigua, the colonial sugar policy fostered a deliberate decision to ignore the educational development of the people. Between 1834 and 1845, the British Government provided what it called "The Negro Education Grant". The Grant was intended to provide basic primary education for the freed

Welcome To Our Beloved
ST. JOHN'S CATHEDRAL
WHICH WAS CONSECRATED ON
25TH OF JULY, 1848.
WE LOOK FORWARD TO OUR
150TH ANNIVERSARY.
PLEASE HELP US IN OUR RESTORATION
FOR THAT GREAT EVENT.
RESTORATION: 2 MILLION
DOLLARS

The twin spires of the Anglican Cathedral of St. John the Divine dominates St. John's. The original wooden structure was built in 1681 and replaced in 1722. A great earthquake in 1843 destroyed the church and re-construction commenced in stone the same year. The interior of the cathedral is encased in wood to protect it from earthquakes and hurricanes. (Inset)An Appeal for funds to help the Cathedral

**Stained glass image in
Holy Family Cathedral, St. John's**

The interior of St. John's Cathedral, which seats about 2000 people, is completely encased in pine timber so as to lessen the effects of earthquakes and hurricanes

Pilgrim Holiness Church

Community Services Centre

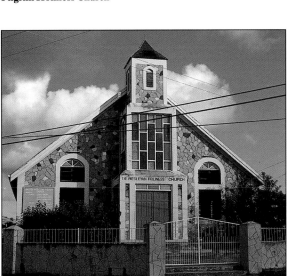

Wesleyan Holiness Church, Swetes

St. Barnabus Church, Liberta

Roman Catholic Church, Tyrells

St. Joseph Roman Catholic Church, St. John's

Two elegant statues, one of John The Divine, the other of John The Baptiste grace the entrance to St. John's Cathedral

Night Service at Spring Gardens Moravian Church, St. John's

Virgin Mary, Holy Family Cathedral, St. John's

On Good Fridays each year, Catholics enact The Stations of the Cross from the village of All Saints to the church at Tyrells

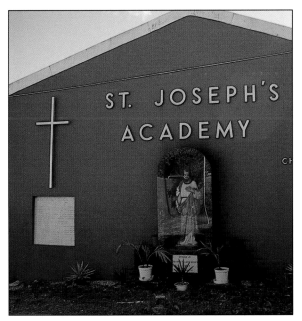

St. Joseph's Academy

Teacher and student

Playing fields at St. Mary's Parish

ABOVE: Today, education is compulsory in Antigua & Barbuda

LEFT: A modern state school

slaves and in 1845 it was discontinued as a lever to force the local legislature to provide education facilities on the island. The legislature, dominated by the sugar barons, saw no benefit in educating workers needed for their fields and therefore, they simply ignored education altogether. For the next 69 years until 1914, it was the churches which provided basic education for the masses of the people. Finally, in 1914, the legislature agreed to assume responsibility for primary education only and though there were secondary schools for a privileged few - the children of the well-to-do - not a single secondary school was introduced for the masses until the 1950's when, as a result of trade

union agitation black people formed the majority in the legislature. Consequently, Antigua has not been able to develop a big enough reservoir of professional skills and now experiences a shortage of skilled and qualified personnel to perform the functions necessary to a growing economy.

Sugar prices began to decline in the 1950's and by the mid-1960's, the industry was in serious financial trouble. The Government was forced to inject $1m simply to keep it afloat and to protect the jobs of some 3,000 workers. But still the Sugar Syndicate would not dispose of the land to Antiguan buyers. It was not until 1967, when sugar was fetching poor prices, that the Syndicate decided to

Diamond Estate: It takes three months, from seed, for yellow and red peppers to ripen

Attempts to grow enough sugar to meet local demand proved too expensive and the projects were stopped

Diamond Estate Farm: A former sugar plantation, now grows and exports sweet potatoes to the United Kingdom. The farm also produces peppers and onions for the local markets

ABOVE: In many countries throughout the Caribbean one-crop sugar cane was replaced by one-crop bananas

LEFT: Lots of skill and hard work is needed to be a coconut man

TOP LEFT: Okra crop
TOP RIGHT: Alexander Mingo, supervisor at Diamond Estate
ABOVE: Sugar cane
BOTTOM : Agricultural project in the east of Antigua

sell. However, even their decision to sell underscored their contempt for the mass of people in Antigua. One estate, Fitches Creek, was earmarked for sale to retired South Africans to be used as residences. The Government had to quickly intervene to stop this plan by pointing out that it was opposed to the system of apartheid in South Africa and had ceased all trading with that country. The Government borrowed over £6m from a Commercial Bank and purchased all the estates.

To protect the jobs of the workers, safeguard the livelihood of peasant cane farmers and avoid importation of sugar, the Government maintained the sugar estates until 1971 when they were closed down, leaving 60 per cent of Antigua's arable land uncultivated.

Since then, the Government has attempted to diversify the agricultural base of the economy by utilising the land for the production of corn/sorghum, cotton and food crops.

In the early 1980s an attempt was made to reintroduce sugar production for domestic consumption, but the memories of worker exploitation in sugar's interest was ingrained in the minds of Antiguans; they would not return to the industry and foreign labour had to be imported. In addition, the costs of rehabilitating the factory and fields were too expensive. The experiment quickly died.

Sugar's legacy proved to be too bitter for Antigua.

Dawn of a New Day

In the first century of the post-emancipation period, the people of Antigua and Barbuda suffered from extreme poverty and neglect. Only minimal attention was given to the economic and social well-being of the workers. The legislative assembly was controlled by the planters who also controlled the government. Laws were passed by the planters for the planters, and the majority of the people were their victims. They had no vote, little right of redress for grievances and even less hope of peacefully changing the situation.

The response of the workers to their low wages and bad conditions of employment was work stoppages or strikes. And, when strikes were outlawed by the planters' laws, sabotage took their place - fields were burnt and estate equipment was destroyed. In 1918, a riot ensued during which 15 people were shot, 12 females and three male. Three of them - two men and a woman - subsequently died.

Workers' resentment to the appallingly poor wages paid for long hours of work, inadequate medical attention and unhygienic living conditions continued to fester for decades. But, in the 1930s when the bottom dropped out of the economy because of poor prices for sugar on the world market, Antigua was ready for violent change. Novelle Richards, an eye witness to these events, described the situation as follows:

> "The island had staked everything on sugar and it was not only bad prices that had to be faced but the inevitable drought that resulted in disastrous crops. Antigua was a land of misery and depression, an island of slums and hovels, of barefooted, unkempt people."

Appalling conditions for workers were not unique to Antiguans and Barbudans - they existed throughout the West Indies. Everywhere the workers reacted in the same way - strikes, sabotage and riots.

Forced to deal with a cauldron of discontent, the British Government dispatched a Commission under Lord Moyne to investigate conditions in the West Indies. What they saw horrified them. In Antigua, they found that wages were atrocious ranging around four pence a day for women and ten pence for men. Workers toiled long and arduous hours from six in the morning to six at night. At some villages, the Commission was witness to desperate conditions - homes were built of wattle cut from bush, and trash from the field covered the roof. Floors were often just the earth. In some villages and particularly in the poorer areas around St John's, there was great

This picture probably taken in the 1930s shows a street in St. John's. Both the houses and the road are in extremely poor condition

A 'Wattle and Daub' worker's house 1939

"Of all the islands in the Westindies, Antigua was possibly the hardest hit by the fall in the sugar market. It had staked everything on sugar and it was not only low prices that had to be faced but also the inevitable drought that resulted in disastrous crops."

From the Commemorative Brochure to mark the 50th Anniversary of the Antigua Trade and Labour Union, January 1939-1989, Hansib Publishing

A view of St. John's with Rat Island in the background taken in the early 1930s. 'Wattle and daub' houses are evident. Since then, much of the area around Rat Island has been reclaimed from the sea and now accommodates Deep Water Harbour

View of St. John's, probably around the 1930s. St. John's Cathedral can be seen in the background
Photo courtesy of Ron Sanders

"The Westindies seethed with unrest. From Jamaica to Trinidad it was poverty, poverty and more poverty. In the islands where sugar was the staple and only industry, mass unemployment was the order of the day. The crops suffered severely from bad prices and, as would be expected, wages were abysmally low."

From the Commemorative Brochure to mark the 50th Anniversary of the AntiguaTrade and Labour Union, January 1939-1989, Hansib Publishing

FAR LEFT: Reginald St. Clair Stevens - Legislator, Jeweller and Trade Union Leader, First President Antigua Trades and Labour Union 1939-1943

LEFT: A young V. C. Bird in his Salvation Army uniform

overcrowding with as many as eight people living in one small house. Windows were eaten by termites as were doors. Crocus bags were used at night to cover doorways and windows to protect against insects.

Staggered by these terrifying conditions, one of the members of the Commission, Sir Walter Citrine held a public meeting in the Anglican Cathedral school room in St John's on 3 January 1939. Citrine was then President of the Trade Union Council in Britain. He urged the formation of a trade union movement to organise the labour force and secure their rights. On 16 January 1939 an Executive was elected to form the Union. It was not, however, until 3 March 1940 that the union was registered under the name Antigua Trades and Labour Union (AT&LU). Reginald Stevens, a jeweller, was the initial president of the body.

That meeting marked the dawn of a new day in the history of Antigua. It was the point at which the veil of slavery and exploitation, which had hung over the Antiguans for three centuries was finally lifted, and the people began to look forward to genuine citizenship in a free society.

It also launched the career of a man who would dominate every aspect of Antiguan and Barbudan life for the next 50 years. Vere Cornwall Bird was

elected as an executive member of the AT&LU at that fateful meeting on 16 January. A former Salvation Army Captain and then small businessman, Bird was elevated to the Presidency of the Union in 1943. He was subsequently to become the first Chief Minister in 1961, the first Premier in 1967, and the first Prime Minister when, on 1 November 1981, Antigua and Barbuda attained full independence from Britain.

Within three months the Union's membership numbered 3,000 and by 1956 its 44 branches in industry and trade totalled 12,712 due-paying members including domestic servants, tradesmen, shop owners, teachers, civil servants and peasant farmers.

In 1946, the Union, under Bird's leadership, recognised that while organised labour had achieved better conditions for workers, change was limited since political authority rested in the Executive Council which was dominated by the plantocrats. A candidate for a parliamentary seat at that time was required to be a property owner. Fortunately for the Union it could produce people with the necessary qualification and in the 1946 General Elections it ran five candidates all of whom were duly elected. Those men were V C Bird,

Edmund H. Lake, elected in the General Elections of 1946 with five other AT&LU members

Ernest Emmanuel Williams is a hero of Antigua and Barbuda's national development. He was a founder member of the Antigua Trades and Labour Union in 1939, and served in parliament from 1946 until he retired in 1984. When the ALP lost the 1971 election, he was leader of the opposition in Parliament. Throughout Antigua, he was loved and respected as a decent man who sought to do his best for his people

E H Lake, E Williams, Leonard Benjamin and Hugh O. Pratt. Despite the fact that five union representatives were elected, only one, V C Bird, was selected to serve on the Executive Council but "while his views were respected, very few of his suggestions were implemented." The Union, however, was determined to place political power in the hands of the people and agitated for constitutional reform. By 1951 there was full adult suffrage in Antigua without qualification of income or literacy test. The Union selected eight candidates to contest the elections and all won their seats.

In 1956, a ministerial system of government was introduced and in the General Elections of the year, the union again won all eight of the elective seats. However, this election was significant because it saw the rise of a new political party of professional Antiguans who had graduated from universities abroad. The party made no impression on the electorate. In elections in 1961 and 1966, these professionals emerged in parties of different names, but the result was the same; solid rejection by the electorate.

1961 saw further constitutional advances for Antigua with the elected membership of the Legislative Council increasing from eight to ten and the position of Chief Minister being created. The Union won all the elected seats easily and for the first time Barbuda was made a constituency. Prior to 1961, Barbuda was attached to St. John's as one constituency. V C Bird was appointed Chief Minister and the pathway to Antigua's independence was cleared.

Conditions in the country had improved during this time, as a result of the trade union's militancy: a fact which was noted by Sir Kenneth Blackburne, Governor of the Leeward Island from 1950 to 1957, in a speech to the Antigua Legislature six years after his arrival:

> "All of us who were in Antigua when the last council was opened five years ago can remember the conditions under which the people of this island were then living. We can remember the trickle of muddy water which emerged intermittently and reluctantly from our clogged pipes; when the children in our schools could not sit down because of lack of room; when there was here in St. John's, rows of filthy hovels in which human beings were living in indescribable conditions."

"In Antigua wages were atrocious ranging from around four pence a day for women and ten pence a day for men"

From the findings of the British Government Moyne Commission 1938

By 1965, the island had made sufficient progress for its leaders to consider independence for Antigua and Barbuda. At this time, there was still only one trade union - the AT&LU - and it was the union representative who formed the Government. In a manifesto for the 1965 General Elections, the union representatives declared their intention to seek independence for Antigua and stated that neither the size of the country nor population constituted an obstacle. The people, once again, gave the union leaders overwhelming support and every seat was won including Barbuda whose representative was McChesney George. In the new Government established by V C Bird, McChesney George was appointed Minister without Portfolio and given responsibility for development in Barbuda.

A Constitutional Conference was held in London in 1966, attended by an Antiguan Government delegation led by V C Bird and including McChesney George. From this conference Antigua with its dependencies Barbuda and Redonda became an Associated State in February 1967. Under this system Antigua was entirely independent in all its internal affairs, but foreign affairs and defence remained under the control of the British. Thus ended over 300 years of colonialism: the people of Antigua

At the 16 January, 1939, meeting, the first elected Executive members of the newly formed Antigua Trades and Labour Union were;
Reginald S. Stevens - President
Barkley A. Richards - General Secretary
F. O. Benjamin - Treasurer
V. C. Bird - Member
Griffith Matthew - Member
Randolph H. Lockhart - Member
Thomas Martin - Member
James Jarvis - Member
C. A. Perry - Member
Thomas Brookes - Member

General Secretaries of the Antigua Trades and Labour Union (AT&LU) from foundation in 1939 to 1994;
Barkley A. Richards
Hugh O. Pratt
Lionel Hurst
George H. Walter
Adolphus E. Freeland
Tanny Rose
Wiggley George
Robin Bascus
Noel Thomas
Senator Natalie Payne

Presidents of the Antigua Trades and Labour Union 1939-1994;
Reginald St. Clair Stevens - 1939/43
Vere Cornwall Bird - 1943/68
Lionel Hurst - 1968/75
Joseph Lawrence - 1976/79
William Robinson - 1979/present

and Barbuda were free to conduct their affairs as they saw fit.

Two developments later occurred which threw the country into turmoil. First some of the leaders on Barbuda led by McChesney George, who had been dismissed from the AT&LU by the Executive, began to agitate for the separation of Barbuda from Antigua. The consequences of this will be detailed later in this section.

Second, between 1967 and 1971, Antigua and Barbuda experienced a political upheaval which broke the hold of the AT&LU. In the mid 1950s, opposition to Bird and the Union emerged amongst the professional and business classes who fielded

Leonard Tim Hector became an Executive member of the AWU and was Chairman of the Progressive Labour Movement and is now Editor of the *Outlet* newspaper and a Senator

George Walter (seated second from left), then Premier and leader of the Progressive Labour Movement with the Government and Opposition following his party's victory in the 1971 General Elections

candidates in the elections of 1956, 1961 and 1966 but were roundly defeated at all of them. However, in 1968, the solidarity amongst the working class, which was the backbone of Bird's strength, ended with the formation of the Antigua Workers Union (AWU) by disgruntled members of the AT&LU, led by its former General Secretary, George Walter. A new political face also appeared on the scene at this time, Leonard Tim Hector. He became an Executive member of the AWU and when the union created a political party, the Progressive Labour Movement (PLM), Hector was made Chairman. He was instrumental in planning and organising a demonstration against the Government in 1968 on recognition for the AWU. Hector resigned a year later saying that the party had campaigned on a policy statement he had devised, but they then abandoned it for expediency. In 1970, George Walter was elected leader of the PLM and in 1971 it won the general elections. Walter became Premier.

The defeat of V C Bird and his band of trade union leaders was surprising. Much had obviously been done to improve conditions in Antigua: workers were receiving better wages, tourism and some manufacturing had been attracted to the cz and a deep water harbour had been built as had an airstrip

capable of accepting modern jet aircraft. Two issues appeared to be the cause of V C Bird's defeat: first, the Government had been forced to buy the sugar estates that were facing closure by the Syndicate of private owners. The AT&LU represented the workers and Walter, as General Secretary, faced the brunt of demands for more pay. However, as Head of the Government, Bird knew that increased wages were not possible in an industry that was attracting only poor prices. The conflict between government, as the employer, and the union, as the workers representative, could not be reconciled. The workers chose to support Walter. In so doing, they joined forces with the business and professional class who had long opposed the AT&LU -the combination undid the AT&LU's electoral chances.

The PLM, however, served only one term in office. The term coincided with unprecedented high prices for oil which affected tourism and sent the country's import bills sky-rocketing - the effect was devastating. Few governments, especially new and inexperienced ones, survive such economic ill fortune. The sugar industry was closed down on the basis that it had become uneconomic to operate; an oil refinery established in 1965 was shut down; and tourism, which the Bird Government had been

(Left to right): Lester Bird, Hugh Marshall, John St. Luce

nurturing since 1960, also slumped. But apart from the economic collapse, the PLM passed legislation which provided its opponents with a rallying point. Among the legislation were the **Public Order Act** which effectively put an end to opposition political activity, and the **Newspaper Amendment Act**, which closed down every newspaper in the country and stifled freedom of expression and speech.

These policies attracted vocal opposition from a new breed of men in the AT&LU and from Tim Hector who had become the leader of the Antigua Caribbean Liberation Movement (ACLM), a party he had helped to form.

It was during this period of the PLM Government that the ALP began to constitute itself as a genuine political party. At a convention in 1972, Lester Bird - second son of V C Bird - was elected Chairman, with John St Luce as General Secretary. Lester Bird had returned from London as an Attorney; John St Luce was a graduate of the London School of Economics. V C Bird remained political Leader and Ernest Emmanuel Williams led the Party in Parliament.

The principal organisers of the ALP were Lester Bird, John St Luce and Hugh Marshall. Since his return to Antigua in 1970, Lester Bird had established a good reputation as a lawyer and was elected as President of the Antigua Cricket Association where his organisational skills became apparent as did his gift for amiability. Along with Marshall and St Luce, he carried the political fight to the Government organising opposition and voicing dissent through Radio ZDK which was owned by the Bird family.

By 1974, a right-wing political party - the Antigua Progressive Party - led by Rowan Henry merged with the ALP and produced a broad-based political party whose membership transcended the AT&LU to include businessmen and professionals. Thus, after three decades of being an appendage of the AT&LU, the ALP had finally come into its own and a period of consolidation followed. However, Rowan Henry was tragically murdered by his gardener on 25 June 1975 before he had a chance to bring the full weight of his personality and reputation to bear on the ALP.

On 3 February 1976, Parliament was dissolved and General Elections were set for 18 February. There followed an intense period of campaigning with both the PLM and ALP confident of victory. During this campaign the ALP undertook to abolish personal income tax in the event of their election.

V. C. Bird Senior in his early twenties. He was to become a Captain in the Salvation Army, President of the AT&LU, and the first Chief Minister, Premier and Prime Minister of Antigua and Barbuda

At King's House, Jamaica.

Admiralty House
Whitehall, S.W. 1

March 31, 1961

My dear Chief Minister

    My wife and I much enjoyed our visit
to Antigua and I was very grateful to you for
your welcome, and I was glad to have the
opportunity of talking to you and the other
members of the Executive Council.

    I enclose a photograph in case you may
like to have it as a small memento of a
visit which I shall always remember with the
greatest pleasure.

Yours very sincerely,
Winston Churchill

The Hon. V.C. Bird.

Letter written to V. C. Bird Snr by Winston Churchill from Jamaica, although the letterhead is Churchill's London home at the time

When former British War time Prime Minister, Winston Churchill, visited Antigua in 1961, he was greeted by Governor, Sir Kenneth Blackburne and V. C. Bird Snr then Chief Minister (right)

Eric Burton, representative of Barbuda in parliament at the time of Antigua's bid for independence in 1981. In the 1984 general election, he became leader of the opposition in parliament and symbolised Barbuda's great influence in the country's affairs at the time. He subsequently lost the Barbuda Constituency to Hilbourn Frank, another Barbudan

Reuben Henry Harris

Vere Bird Jnr

This was obviously of great attraction to the electorate and in combination with some of the more unpopular actions of the PLM, the ALP became irresistible to a large group of people. Hence on 19 February, the ALP had won ten seats, the PLM five, the Barbuda seat went to an independent, and there was a tie in the constituency of St. Phillips North where the candidates were Reuben Harris for the ALP and Edison Lewis for the PLM. The Court later gave the seat to Reuben Harris upon examination of disputed ballots.

What was remarkable about the election, however, is that while the ALP won eleven seats it received only 49.0 per cent of the vote, a slightly lower share than the losing PLM's 49.9 per cent.

As Leader of the ALP, V C Bird became Premier and appointed the Chairman of the Party, Lester Bird, to the post of Deputy Premier. Vere Bird Jnr, the eldest of V C Bird's sons and partner with Lester in the law firm of Bird & Bird, also won a seat in the Elections. Thus, was born a charge of "the Bird dynasty" in Antiguan politics

When the ALP returned to office in 1976, in an attempt to stave-off secessionist forces on Barbuda, one of its first legislative actions was to pass an Act of Parliament establishing the Barbuda Local

Government Council and giving it broad powers to conduct the local affairs of Barbuda.

Barbuda and Antigua had always experienced an awkward relationship, which is perhaps best captured by a phrase in a memorandum submitted by the Parliamentary Representative of Barbuda, Mr Eric Burton to the British Secretary of State of Foreign and Commonwealth Affairs in 1980. He described the perception of Barbudans in relation to Antigua as a "subtle feeling of neglect, inferiority, frustration and suppression which pervades the mind of every Barbudan."

The prevailing attitudes, however, did not manifest themselves in division between the two communities until 1967, when McChesney George, the representative of Barbuda in the Legislature and Minister of the Antigua Government split away from his old friend, V C Bird, the Chief Minister of Antigua. George promoted the idea of secession among the Barbudans, stressing that the community had been neglected by the Antiguan Government. On 8 and 9 December 1967, 25 policemen were sent from Antigua to Barbuda because V C Bird felt that George was "stirring up trouble". In 1968, George made a statement to the committee of 24 at the United Nations pressing a case for

Members of the First Associated State's Cabinet. (Left to right): Premier, V. C. Bird; Deputy Premier, Lionel A. Hurst; Ministers: E. E. Williams, E. H. Lake and McChesney George

Barbuda's secession from Antigua. The Government was sufficiently concerned about the effects of McChesney George's activity to commission a study "on the development potential of the Island of Barbuda, with a view to realising that potential."

In a memorandum submitted to the British Government during the independence negotiations in December 1980, the Antigua Government stated that "the ALP Government began implementation of many of the recommendations of the (study) but could not continue the programme since it lost the General Election in 1971."

George's secessionist activity did not find fertile ground immediately. This was demonstrable when he contested the Barbuda seat in the 1971 General Elections as an independent and was defeated by the PLM candidate, Claude Earl Francis, who was also a Barbudan. However, while the majority of Barbudans may have voted for Francis, George still had a vociferous following for his secessionist ideas and created enough discontent on the island to encourage the PLM Government to send police to Barbuda more than once. In a dramatic presentation to the British Foreign Office, the Barbudan Parliamentary representative, Eric Burton, described the PLM Government's attitude to Barbuda as follows:

"They continued the policy of their predecessors by sending police to Barbuda under the slightest pretext and on one occasion used tear gas and rifle bullets on the islanders because they staged a peaceful demonstration against an oppressive, abusive and tyrannical warden, an Antiguan."

The Barbudans were greatly encouraged by the success of Anguilla in breaking away from the union of St Kitts-Nevis because it felt neglected by the Government in St Kitts. In 1971, after four years of agitation for secession, Anguilla returned to being a British Colony.

With secessionist forces on the ascendency in Barbuda, Claude Earl Francis abandoned the PLM to be elected Parliamentary Representative of Barbuda as an independent. Meanwhile, the newly created Barbuda Council functioned as a voice of dissent for the secessionist Barbudans and became involved in petty disputes with the central Government. In February 1978, Claude Earl Francis died and in a subsequent by-election, Eric Burton was elected to replace him as Barbuda's Parliamentary Representative. He too supported the secessionist cause and it was on that ticket that he was re-elected in the April 1980 General Elections which had the independence of Antigua as its principal theme.

The accusations of Government neglect of Barbuda was addressed by the Antigua Government at the Independence negotiations in London in December 1980. The Government pointed out that among the powers accorded to the Barbuda Council in 1976 was "the right to collect revenues generated locally, such as hotel taxes and commissions on sand mined on Barbuda, and to spend such revenues on programmes and projects for Barbuda." The Government also stated that the five-year period 1971-1976, the PLM administration spent a total of EC$1,271,500 on Barbuda while in the period 1976-1979, the ALP Government spent EC$2,309,000 and this sum did not include the cost of subsidising electricity or sending a medical team to Barbuda weekly. The Government concluded that on a per capita basis Antigua received only $8.00 more than was spent on Barbuda per capita over the period 1976-1979.

The Barbuda secessionists opposed independence

"Their population was 1,200 people and even to their most ardent supporters that independence could not be sustained"

for Antigua if Barbuda was expected to be a part of the State. In what was to become characteristic of their campaign the Barbudans dramatically announced that they "**would prefer death to a union of any sort with Antigua**" They repeatedly told the British High Commissioner that Barbudans wanted one of two things, either separate independence or reversion to British Colonial status as in the case of Anguilla. A most impressive campaign was mounted including lobbies at the British Parliament, the retention of a Queen's Counsel in London and much media coverage. Over time, they abandoned the idea of separate independence. Their population was 1,200 people and even to their most ardent supporters that independence could not be sustained.

The focus of Barbudan concern, therefore became separation from Antigua and a return to British Colonial status though, in his remarks at the opening of the 1980 Constitutional Conference in London on Independence for Antigua, Eric Burton stated, "**we have been told that Her Majesty's Government desires no dependencies. In this**

On the occasion of the State Opening of The Third Session of Parliament on 6 January 1969. (Sitting from left to right): Hon. D. W. Hurst - Speaker; Hon. V .C. Bird - Premier; Sir Wilfred Jacobs K.B., O.B.E., Q.C. - Governor; Hon. Senator W. Burton - President of the Senate; The Very Rev. G. S. Baker - Dean of Antigua. (Standing from left to right): Hon. E. H. Lake; Hon. Senator E. Cochraine; Hon. Senator J. Meade; Hon. B. T. Carrott; Hon. L. Hurst; Hon. J. Lawrence; Hon. Senator C. T. Simon; Hon. D. M. Sheppard; Hon. R. Harris; Hon. S. Prince; Mr. Hull - ADC to Governor; Senator L. Joseph; Hon. G. A. Sheppard; Hon. C. O. R. Phillips (Acting Attorney General); Mr. L. N. Stevens (Clerk of Parliament); Hon. Senator G. O. Watt; Hon. Senator M. Francis; Mr. M. L. Barrow (Chief of Police); Hon. Senator C. Francis; Hon. R. Hall

event, we are prepared to go into full independence on our own."

It was obvious from the outset of the Constitutional Conference that the British Government was not going to facilitate secession by Barbuda. The Chairman of the Conference and head of the British Delegation, Mr Nicholas Ridley, stated: "What we must do - not in the spirit of antagonism and the past - is to try and find if there is a way which will be satisfactory to all to integrate the state of Antigua with the island of Barbuda."

The British had attracted widespread international criticism over Anguilla in 1971. Moreover, Britain was anxiously divesting itself of colonies which were a drain on British taxpayers' money. In these circumstances, the UK Government was determined that Barbuda should not be allowed to secede from Antigua, but they wanted a good face put on it. The Antigua Government was not even entertaining discussion on secession. In its memorandum on Barbuda, the Government stated clearly that "territorial integrity must be paramount to encouraging fragmentation and balkanisation of states."

The Conference devoted nine of its twenty-two plenary sessions to Barbuda alone. In addition there

were a number of informal meetings on particular aspects of the issue in which Sir Richard Posnett, the alternate Chairman of the Conference, steered the Barbuda delegation away from secession and encouraged the Antigua Government delegation towards a greater devolution of authority to the Barbuda Council over Barbudan affairs.

In fact, the solution to the Barbuda issue was found by supreme British diplomacy in alternating between threatening the Barbudans with total abandonment if they persisted with secessionists demands, and cajoling the Antiguan Government into greater concessions. In the end, the matter of secession was dropped altogether and, except for a proposal that an independent body, such as the Commonwealth Secretariat, should be invited to review the operation of the new arrangements, the Government agreed to the devolution of greater powers to the Barbuda Council than they already had under the 1976 Act.

While the Barbudans continued to express dissatisfaction with the outcome of the Conference, they did absolutely nothing in pursuance of secession. On 16 April 1981, the Government amended the 1976 Act giving the Council the powers offered at the London Conference and making the

Sand quarrying in Barbuda

Hilbourne Frank of the Barbudan Council

island virtually self-governing. The Act was signed by the Governor-General, Sir Wilfred Jacobs, on 7 May 1981. The powers of the Council go beyond those of any Local Government anywhere in the world and include responsibilities as follows:

    (a) to administer agriculture and forestry;

    (b) to administer public health, medical and sanitary facilities and services;

    (c) to administer and regulate the provision of electricity and water services and other public utilities;

    (d) to construct, improve and maintain roads;

    (e) to raise and collect revenue pursuant to the provisions of this Act to enable the Council to meet expenses necessarily incurred or to be incurred in the performance of its powers and functions under this sub-section except to the extent that financial provision may be made from time to time by Parliament.

The Council was also given the duties of **"promoting hotel and tourist development in accordance with and subject to any law relating to the alienation of land, foreign investment or tax incentives"**; and administering fisheries. In other words, apart from the control of land and security forces on the island, the Barbuda Council was accorded full control. The extent of the devolution of power to the Council was described as "**unprecedented in our experience**" by the British Government, whose spokesman pointed out that there were two constitutional safeguards for these powers:

> **"First, no Bill to alter Section 123 of the independence constitution which relates to the Barbuda Council can receive assent without approval of both Houses of Parliament and of a two-thirds majority referendum. Secondly, no bill relating to the Barbuda Local Government Act, which defines the Council's powers, can be regarded as being passed until it receives the consent of the Barbuda Council. Amendment by the Senate must similarly receive the Council's consent before amendment."**

Further, the Government wrote into the Independence Constitution, the right of the Barbuda Council to appoint a Senator to the Upper House of Parliament. For, two and a half years afterwards, the Barbuda Council did not exercise their right to appoint a member of the Senate of Parliament, but following the 1984 General Elections, Hilbourn Frank was nominated by the Council after he

"Barbuda and Antigua had always experienced an awkward relationship, which is perhaps best captured by a phrase in a memorandum submitted by the Parliamentary Representative of Barbuda, Mr Eric Burton to the British Secretary of State of Foreign and Commonwealth Affairs in 1980. He described the perception of Barbudans in relation to Antigua as a 'subtle feeling of neglect, inferiority, frustration and suppression which pervades the mind of every Barbudan.'"

In 1966, Antigua sought independence from Britain. At a Constitutional Conference in London, V. C. Bird Snr, states his government's case. Pictured left is David Rose, a Guyanese, Administrator of Antigua and right is Edmund H. Lake, then a Minister

unsuccessfully challenged Eric Burton for the Barbuda seat. Barbuda had achieved influence not only over its own affairs, but also over national decision-making in the country. However, while talk of secession has virtually ended, relations between the Government and the Council remain volatile as each attempts to assert what it regards as its legitimate authority.

As a post script to the Barbuda secession episode it is worth noting that, at the 1980 Constitutional Conference in London, the Government had proposed that the name of the independent state should be "Antigua-Barbuda". It was McChesney George who insisted on "Antigua and Barbuda".

After the ALP's return to office in 1976, the economy of the country turned around. Between 1977 and 1979, the economy grew by an average of eight per cent. New hotels were constructed, manufacturing enterprises mushroomed and employment increased. The Government boasted of its achievements which included:

-an increase in earnings for tourism workers from EC$4 million in 1974 to EC$$9.6 million in 1979

-an improvement in bank deposits from EC$64 million in 1973 to EC$131 million in 1979

-a hike in civil servants salaries from EC$15 million in 1973 to EC$38 million in 1979; and

-an expansion of factories from five in 1973 to 17 in 1979.

Lester Bird put the issue of independence to a convention of the ALP in September 1978, and he advocated it forcefully. He said:

"We would make a mockery of all the rebellions of our forefathers who, either individually or collectively, recognized our inherent right to be free of the British; we would cast a stigma on our children and their children when they learn after years of leading the way to freedom, Antigua did not have the courage to tear itself away from Britain and proudly say... We are free, we are our own masters, we are an independent nation."

The response of the convention was overwhelmingly in support of Lester Bird's call for independence. In its manifesto for the 1980 general election, the ALP stated that it "will immediately seek independence." By the time of the elections, independence was virtually a non-issue. The ACLM declared in its Manifesto that the "ACLM

At the 1966 Constitutional talks in London which led to Antigua becoming the first Associated State in the Caribbean 1967. V. C. Bird Snr (centre) with Donald Halsted (later to become a member of the opposition) and Arthur Bottomley (right) the British Minister for Commonwealth Affairs

V. C. Bird Snr

unreservedly supports national independence for Antigua and Barbuda" and the PLM said it "has the personnel and expertise to lead Antigua into independence and the PLM has the will to work for a united front to develop an independent Antigua."

Opposition to the ALP crumbled at the 1980 general election. The party won 13 of the 17 seats, with only three going to the PLM and Barbuda returning an independent candidate. Everyone regarded this as a clear manifestation of the support by the Antiguan people for independence from Britain. Eight months later, the Antigua and British Governments met - with representatives of the PLM and Barbuda present - at Lancaster House in London to decide the Constitution of an independent Antigua.

Apart from Barbuda, which was the most contentious issue, the matters for discussion at the Conference centred on a few of the clauses in the draft Constitution prepared by the Antigua Government. Although the PLM delegation had argued strongly for the inclusion of provisions with respect to the right to strike, the right to collective bargaining and the collection of union dues, they identified the "main failure of the Conference" as **"the failure satisfactorily to resolve the Barbuda situation." Both the PLM and Barbuda delegates**

declined to sign the report despite the fact that they had "participated throughout the Conference and in the preparation of the report."

In June 1981, the Government introduced the Antigua and Barbuda Constitution Order 1981 and on 31 July 1981, Her Majesty The Queen signed the Order at Buckingham Palace in London.

On 31 October 1981, Princess Margaret, as the Queen's Representative, handed over the instruments of independence to V C Bird, Premier of Antigua, before a crowd estimated as half the population. (*The speech delivered by V C Bird at the state banquet preceding the proclamation of Independence appears in the Appendix*).

At midnight, the Union Jack was lowered for the first time in 328 years. As Prime Minister, V C Bird spoke to the independent nation of Antigua and Barbuda, he said:

> "The ultimate safeguard of
> independence is productivity. This
> nation, born again tonight must commit
> itself to work and to work hard. For if
> we fail to do so, the consequence of our
> failure will be dependence on a new
> master who will, once again, dictate our
> policies and direct our affairs. We must

Prime Minister V. C. Bird receives constitutional instruments from Her Royal Highness Princess Margaret. (Inset) Princess Margaret delivering the 'Throne Speech' as representative of Her Majesty The Queen at the State Opening of the first Parliament of independent Antigua and Barbuda on 2 November 1981

The Government at Independence

Vere C Bird Snr
Prime Minister

Lester B Bird
Deputy Prime Minister
Minister for External
Affairs, Economic
Development,
Tourism & Energy

Keith Ford
Attorney General
and Minister of Legal
Affairs

Christopher O'Mard
Minister of Health

Ernest E Williams
Minister of Works,
Communications &
Public Utilities

John E St Luce
Minister of Finance

Adolphus Freeland
Minister of Labour
& Social Security

Vere Bird Jnr
Adviser to
Prime Minister

Joseph Myers
Minister of Local
Government

Donald C Christian
Minister in Ministry
of Education

Reuben Harris
Minister of Education,
Youth & Culture

Robin Yearwood
Minister of
Agriculture

Hilroy Humphries
Parliamentary
Secretary in Ministry of
Economic Development
& Tourism

Hugh C Marshall
Minister of
Information

Senator Lionel Hurst
Minister in Ministry
of Public Works

Courtesy of the Official Independence Magazine, 1 November 1981

not have struggled so long and with such fortitude to exchange one master for another."

In a telling exchange at the conclusion of his speech, Princess Margaret remarked to V C Bird that she had not realised that he had felt so passionately about the need to be free from Britain. V C Bird's reply was a polite but deafening silence.

On 1 November the Antiguan flag was raised for the first time.(*The speech delivered by V C Bird at the Flag Raising ceremony appears in the Appendix*). On the morning of 2 November 1981 at a joint session of the Senate and the House of Assembly, Princess Margaret delivered a speech from the Throne setting out the Government's policy for the new nation of Antigua and Barbuda. She said:

"Above all else the human rights and freedoms of the people of Antigua and Barbuda are held sacrosanct by my Government. The Constitution safeguards these rights particularly freedom of speech, of the press and of assembly. In ensuring that the Constitutional provisions are upheld, my Government will pay special attention to the rights of liberty, property, security and legal redress of grievances."

The new-born nation of Antigua and Barbuda was ready to embark on the adventure of full independence. Nine days later, on 11 November 1981, Antigua and Barbuda took its seat at the United Nations during the 36th General Assembly. Lester Bird, as Foreign Minister, made his country's international posture clear:

"My Country, Antigua and Barbuda, is a small State. We have no military

The Men
of Labour

The Men of Labour sowed the seeds
Of self-respect and pride;
With toil and sweat, they nurtured thee,
They braved the surging tide;
Those men of labour stood the grind,
They fought courageously;
Colonial Masters tried but failed,
To stun their victory.

Nine months of savage pressure bore,
No man did yield one inch;
Starvation was the weapon mean,
Each man did feel the pinch:
But victory was the goal from start,
"No going back" they said;
Strong will and steadfast grit they showed
"We'll fight till all are dead".

Brave Reggie Stevens lit the torch;
He passed it on with pride;
Bird, Williams, Lake and all the rest,
Working side by side:
The task was tedious, rough and tough:
It seemed no end was near,
But victory was the goal for all,
From week to month to year.

Renewed with vigour, strength and heart,
The Movement grew and grew;
Vere Cornwall Bird now at the helm,
The fight was fierce and true;
The soldiers came, wild fires raged,
But no retreat – no! no!
Push forward further in the fight,
Our progress sure but slow.

The decades came and went quite fast,
The victories mounted high;
The right to organise secured,
The limit was the sky;

In politics, Labour triumphed too,
The right to vote was earned,
To Council Labour men did go,
True self-respect returned.

So fifty years of honest toil,
A firm foundation laid;
Let's build upon this structure sure,
The sacrifice was made.
We cannot – dare not – fail the test,
The future's ready made;
By men of courage; grit and zeal,
We stand now in their shade.

Vere Cornwall Bird, Chief Minister first,
First Premier statesman, too;
First Prime Minister, now, is he,
The Nation's proud of you:
For all these fifty years and more,
You've served your country well;
Through thick and thin, you stood quite firm,
No words enough to tell.

With heartfelt thanks and gratitude,
This nation now expresses
Its love and admiration, Sir,
To you and all the rest;
One golden era now is passed,
We must take up the fight;
All bitter wrangling, hate and greed
Must now be put to flight.

Renewed commitment we must make,
To strengthen what was done,
At home, in school, at work, at play;
This task has just begun;
Antiguans and Barbudans all,
Behind our Leader stand;
May truth and honesty flow free,
Throughout this blessed Land.

Thank God for V.C. Bird and those
Who took the mantle then,
To open wide the Gates of Hope,
Those special chosen men:
They all will wear their golden crown,
As round God's Throne they stand,
"Come ye dear children", he will say,
Stand close at My right hand.

Ivor B. Ford

**ABOVE: The Official Independence
Magazine, 1 November 1981**

LEFT: *The Men of Labour* **by Ivor B. Ford,
reproduced from the Commemorative
Brochure for the 50th Anniversary of the
Antigua Trade and Labour Union, 1989. The
poem is dedicated to those who led the
struggle for Independence**

**muscle and want none, we have no
quarrels with neighbours or nations
further afield and we wish to keep it
so. Our most earnest desire is a
world secure in peace and stability; a
world where man fulfils his obligation to
the survival of his fellow man
above the narrow concerns of
ideology, above racial prejudice and
above religious bigotry.**"

In the years after independence, the "challenge
of the PLM - the only party ever to defeat the ALP
- dissipated." In 1984, the PLM received only a
minuscule vote and the ALP won all the Antigua
seats. The lone opposition in parliament came from
the independent Barbuda representative.

Opposition to the Government galvanized outside
of parliament, principally in the **Outlet Newspaper,**
an ACLM publication edited by Leonard Tim
Hector, the party's leader. By the time of the 1989
election, the PLM had disintegrated and many of its
former members with the support of the Antigua
Workers Union formed the United National
Democratic Party (UNDP) with a surgeon, Dr Ivor
Heath, as its leader. The UNDP performed
creditably achieving 31 per cent of the votes, but
securing only one seat in parliament. Shortly after,
the opposition forces - UNDP and ACLM - decided
to merge in order to try to wrest power from the
ALP. The President of the AWU, Baldwyn Spencer,
was elected leader of the party.

As the end of the twentieth century approached
and V C Bird reached his eighties, the ALP sought a
new leader in 1992 - the first such attempt in 49
years. The contestants to replace V C Bird were
Lester Bird and John E St Luce - the two men

Antigua's *The Nation* newspaper, 29 May 1992

Baldwin Spencer, Leader of the Opposition since 1989

John St. Luce, candidate in the leadership race for the Antigua Labour Party

Tim Hector, Editor of Antigua's *Outlet* newspaper, galvanising support in opposition to the government

who had returned from their studies in England in 1968 to breathe new life into the ALP during its only period of opposition. When the result of the ballot by 300 delegates was announced at the ALP convention, no victor had emerged - Bird and St Luce had tied with 150 votes each.

A year passed before another convention was held. In September 1993, Lester Bird defeated John E St Luce to become the second leader of the ALP in 50 years.

The mantle of leadership passed to a new generation - in government and in opposition. History will tell what they make of their inheritance.

Lester Bird had urged independence for Antigua and Barbuda to a party convention in 1978. On 11 November 1981, he delivered the first address by his country to the United Nations

"We are lucky that we still have alive the Rt. Hon. Prime Minister Vere Cornwall Bird, who lived and served through this entire period for the most part as the leader of this movement, and we should therefore, I believe, put aside parties, politics and personalities and understand that we are a part of history and that we should ensure that as such we pay enough respect to it so that others from outside will respect what we have achieved. "

Lester Bird, 50th Anniversary of the Antigua Trade and Labour Union, 1989

"We are guilty of not addressing the affairs of our old people sufficiently. Although we have a contributory pension fund and a senior citizens' institute, these are not enough in present times. People who have served our country must, at the end of their days, still feel valuable. "

Lester Bird, speaking after his election victory as Leader of The Antigua Labour Party, 1993

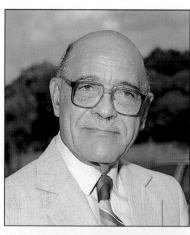

Joseph Myers, MP, St Peters. Will not be contesting the 1994 election

Henderson S. Simon, MP, St John's City West

Aldolphus Freeland, MP, St George's

Hilroy Humphreys, MP, All Saints West

Robin Yearwood, MP, St Philip's North

Molwyn Joseph, MP, St Mary's North

Eustace Cochraine, MP, All Saints East and St Luke's

Chris Omarde, MP, St John's City South. Will not be contesting the 1994 election

A royal visit to Antigua: (left to right) H. E. The Right Honorable V. C. Bird, Prime Minister; Her Majesty Queen Elizabeth; H. E. the former Governor-General, Sir Wilfred Jacobs and Mrs W. Jacobs

Keith Forde Q. C.,
Attorney General

The Workers Voice - champion of the people's cause since 1943

Bernard Percival, MP
Minister of Education

50th Anniversary
Commemorative Brochure for
the Antigua Trade and Labour
Union, January 1989,
dedicated to the Union's
founding fathers

PARADISE FOUND

Jumby Bay Club, Long Island

The islands of Antigua and Barbuda are a banquet of beauty; a feast of sunshine, sand and sea to delight the most discriminating gourmet. With over 365 beaches, the twin-islands offer a regimen of water-sports, deep-sea diving, reef exploration, yachting, plentiful fishing and lazy bathing that is without comparison anywhere in the world.

The beaches range from dazzling white to golden sands; the water is warm, gentle and crystal clear. No experience quite matches slumbering on a beach chair, under a coconut tree at sundown as the water softly laps against the shore while the sound of a distant steelband wafts through the air. Paradise indeed; after the dark and chill of European and North American winters.

For centuries this paradise remained unknown to most Europeans and North Americans except for the traveller fascinated by the West Indies. While none of these wanderers failed to endorse the beauty of the islands, it was not until 1949 that the paradise of Antigua was found by a group of millionaires who successfully kept it secret for many years.

This millionaire group with holiday homes in Bermuda sought another more exclusive and remote location for their winter frolics. After much

investigation, they decided upon Antigua and set up the **Mill Reef Club** in 1949. The early membership was impressive and included Paul Mellon and his wife (Exxon Oil), Laurens Hammond (Hammond Organ), Philip Reed former Chairman of General Electric and Henry Ketch the inventor of the cartoon character 'Dennis the Menace'. They constructed an exclusive estate with million dollar homes and private beaches, a common clubhouse, a 9 hole golf course and tennis courts.

Mill Reef Club continues in Antigua as it always has - unintrusively and imperceptibly. While it creates no offence to the Antiguans, the Club and individual members - the Mellons particularly - have been helpful to the community by providing scholarships for University education and contributing to worthy causes such as facilities at the **Holberton Hospital**, a public institution.

When the United States imposed its blockade on Cuba in 1960 after the rise of Fidel Castro, Americans began to look around for other holiday islands in the Caribbean. Many of them, following the lead of the Mill Reefers, found Antigua and started visiting in increasing numbers.

It is small wonder that in the early 1960's, the government of Antigua and Barbuda took

HALF MOON BAY CLUB, Half Moon Bay Beach, is situated at one end of a beautiful crescent shaped bay on the south coast. It has a swimming pool, sunfish, windsurfing, canoeing, snorkelling, tennis and golf. There is lots to do at this All Inclusive hotel

advantage of the islands' natural attractions to promote tourism. From very modest beginnings, the tourist industry is now the most important sector of the economy, contributing 25 per cent to the Gross Domestic Product (GDP).

The country boasts 56 hotels and 47 guest houses and apartments with over a hundred restaurants offering sumptuous cuisine that spreads from exotic local dishes to Italian, French and Swiss-German fayre. Nightclubs and discotheques have mushroomed providing a variety of entertainment but especially the rhythms of calypso and the scintillating beat of the steel band.

Casinos are also available to the tourist who would like to live a little dangerously.

Tourism directly employs 2,350 people, but when the spin-off effect of the industry is calculated, total employment is nearer 5,000. Taxi-drivers, workers in boutiques and other shops, handicraft makers and sellers - all of these also benefit from tourism.

Aside from the beaches, the country offers spectacular sailing. Few pleasures match the sailors delight in leisurely meandering through the blue Caribbean waters sailing to secluded coves and sheltered beaches for a day of quiet bliss. Those who like a "jump up" on the sea, favour cruising on the "**Jolly Roger**", a converted pirate ship, which provides all the booze anyone can drink with good food and music, while it sails the waters off Antigua. Those who prefer exploring the world beneath the sea, are enchanted by the coral reefs and multi-coloured fish that characterise Antiguan and Barbudan waters.

Sport enthusiasts quickly discover the lawn tennis courts and the fact that professional aspirants flock to Antigua for "**Tennis Week**" in January to test their skills against each other and to train for the international circuit. Golf fans are delighted with the 18-hole golf course at **Cedar Valley** and the spectacular 9-hole course at **Half Moon Bay**.

Tourist are visiting Antigua and Barbuda in increasing numbers. In 1976, there were 56,398 visitors, by 1992, over 144,873, and an estimated 400,000 visitors were expected by the end of 1996. Alongside the development of facilities for the tourist and measures to increase the earning of the locals from the industry, the Government has built the modern **V C Bird International Airport**. The airport provides direct connections to Frankfurt, London, Miami, New York and Toronto. In addition, Antigua is the gateway to the Eastern Caribbean and South America with several flights daily to most Caribbean

Graceful palm offering shade at the BLUE WATERS HOTEL

Antigua and Barbuda are surrounded by spectacular reefs - superb for scuba diving and snorkelling

Jolly Roger pirate cruises

V. C. BIRD INTERNATIONAL AIRPORT provides direct links to the Caribbean, Canada, Europe and the United States

ST. JAMES'S CLUB consists of 100 acres set on a sun-drenched peninsula jutting into the Caribbean Sea at Mamora Bay. Leisure facilities include jacuzzi, horseback riding, massage parlour, beauty salon, tennis, water sports, cable television, mini-bars, casino, five boutiques, five bars, laundry service, four pools, four restaurants, room service, exercise room, deep-sea fishing, croquet lawn, two beaches and marina

FALMOUTH BEACH APARTMENTS, Falmouth Harbour, offer fully equipped studios. Close by are restaurants, supermarket, gift shops, bank, post office, Nelson's Dockyard, sports club, massage & beauty salon and beach

**Deep Bay provides almost everything the visitor requires -
just a short stroll from the Ramada Renaissance Royal Antiguan Resort**

HAWKSBILL BEACH RESORT, Five Islands, is set among 39 acres of beachfront property with four beaches - on one beach clothing is optional. The hotel has 95 rooms, plus the Great House, and a deluxe villa situated on a peninsula. The resort boasts award winning cuisine at its two restaurants. There are two cocktail bars, water sports, tennis court, laundry and dry cleaning services. (Inset) Antigua and Barbuda is fast becoming the Caribbean leader in providing a complete wedding and honeymoon service. Each year hundreds of couples experience this top quality package. In 1993, over 200 couples chose Hawksbill Hotel for their wedding and honeymoon. In addition to being pampered and given special treatment, couples receive bonus discounts and a variety of offers on return trips

Cruise ship passengers walk off their ships directly into the heart of St. John's

countries. Further, having been served for years by a deep water harbour, outside of **St John's**, the Government decided to construct an entirely new harbour especially for cruise ships on the very edge of the town. Now, passengers on cruise ships disembark into the heart of **St John's.** In a real sense the new port and Airport symbolise the significance and importance of tourism to the people of Antigua and Barbuda, for while they will serve visitors to the country, equally they will benefit locals. And that, in essence, is what tourism in Antigua and Barbuda is all about - service to the visitors and benefits for the people in an atmosphere of genuine friendliness and warmth.

There are now 3000 rooms available for tourists in Antigua and Barbuda. These include exclusive hotels such as the magnificent **Coco Point Lodge** on Barbuda, the picturesque **Jumby Bay** on Long Island, and the all-inclusive hotel for couples, **Sandals,** which sits on magnificent

Dickenson Bay in Antigua. The **Ramada Renaissance Royal Antiguan** is the country's largest hotel combining all the elements of an idyllic Caribbean holiday with superb conference facilities.

One of the largest hotel resorts in the Caribbean is **Jolly Harbour Beach Resort** situated on 500 acres of land including two fingers which extend into a harbour and man made island. The development includes a hotel, waterfront villas, a marina for 144 berths, a boat building shop, a shopping centre, restaurants, and a golf course. The aim of the developer, Alfred Erhart, was to create a sense of community between vacationers and the local population. Strolling through **Jolly Harbour** certainly gives the impression a sense of community has been achieved.

All beach hotels offer a variety of water sports including water ski-ing, jet ski-ing and wind surfing. Arrangements are also made for scuba diving, deep sea fishing or cruises.

JUMBY BAY, is a 300 acre site situated on a private island two miles north of Antigua. Exclusive, yet accessible it comprises of 38 junior sized suites and 18 luxurious private villas, all with an ocean view of secluded beaches. Leisure facilities include water-skiing, tennis, snorkelling, sunfish sail-boats, sailboards, sunfloats, bicycles, croquet, putting green and bar

JOLLY HARBOUR BEACH RESORT is one of the largest hotel resorts in the Caribbean situated on 500 acres of land

THIS PAGE: RUNAWAY BEACH CLUB, Runaway Bay, situated on a mile-long beach offers beachfront rooms and self-contained villa apartments. Ideally located for shopping in the capital and airport. Facilities include the Lobster Pot waterside restaurant and bar, a freshwater pool, table tennis, pool table, diving centre, water-skiing, casino and golf nearby

COPPER & LUMBER STORE HOTEL, Nelson's Dockyard, English Harbour, has been restored and features 14 suites individually decorated and each named after a ship that fought at the Battle of Trafalgar. Amenities include an English Pub, restaurant, bar, tennis, squash and scuba diving

CLUB ANTIGUA, Jolly Harbour

TIME AWAY BEACH APARTMENTS, Runaway Bay

SANDALS ANTIGUA, located on the shores of Dickenson Bay, close to the airport and the capital. The resort has 207 air-conditioned rooms - in eight categories - with satellite television. On the premises there are dining facilities, two speciality restaurants and a New York deli. Three bars including a swim-up pool bar, four swimming pools and a sing-along piano bar. Full sports facilities complete the package

BLUE HERON HOTEL, Johnson's Point. A secluded resort which is casual yet elegant, featuring superior air-conditioned rooms with balconies and a gourmet restaurant. Water sports available

YEPTON BEACH RESORT, Hog John Bay, has 38 beachfront deluxe rooms, studios and apartments with full kitchens situated on a secluded white sand beach and is close to a casino. Baby sitting arrangements available

RAMADA RENAISSANCE ROYAL ANTIGUAN RESORT, Deep Bay

ANTIGUA VILLAGE CONDOMINIUM BEACH RESORT, Dickenson Bay. Situated among coconut and palm trees on a mile-long stretch of white-sand beach is the Mediterranean-style Village Condominium. Leisure facilities includes a freshwater pool, maid and laundry service, water sports, two beachfront restaurants and nearby bars

HODGES BAY CLUB & CONDOMINIUMS, Hodges Bay. These villas provide an ocean view from private balconies. Tennis courts, swimming pools and water sports facilities complete the package

TRAFALGAR BEACH VILLAS, Pillar Rock Beach, is a complex of air-conditioned one and two room villas on a five acre site that slopes down to a white sand beach

LEFT: CURTAIN BLUFF HOTEL

BELOW: HERITAGE HOTEL located in Heritage Quay Complex, St John's, provides easy access to casinos, shops, restaurants, banks and supermarkets. The hotel caters to the business traveller with studio and air-conditioned suites which are totally self contained. There is a restaurant, meeting rooms and full business services

ABOVE: SAND HAVEN HOTEL, Sand Haven, is located on a private beach in a secluded area and features variable rooms with television. Leisure services includes a restaurant and beach bar

RIGHT: SANDALS ANTIGUA - an old anchor in the forecourt is all that remains of the former Anchorage Hotel

BELOW: JOLLY HARBOUR BEACH RESORT, Jolly Harbour, offers furnished waterfront villas with convenient moorings for boat owners. Leisure facilities include restaurants, bars, freshwater pool, squash court, tennis courts, gym, shopping centre, two beaches, day charters for sailing, diving and water sports

TOP LEFT: AT-THE-HILL RESORT, Marble Hill.
Apartments with a panoramic view of Dickenson Bay and the coast

TOP RIGHT: JOLLY CASTLE HOTEL is a new project with a super location giving access to Joseph's Supermarket, Club Antigua and many local sport and leisure facilities

LEFT: BEACHCOMBER HOTEL located three minutes from the airport and has everything to offer the business traveller and holiday maker from sports facilities to fine dining in an excellent Caribbean setting

ABOVE: ANTIGUA SUGAR MILL HOTEL, Coolidge, is close to the airport and features an authentic 260-year old sugar mill. Facilities provided include free remote control cable television, a freshwater pool, restaurant, games room, laundry service. Facilities for the business traveller include, boardroom, secretarial services/copy services, fax etc

SUNSET VIEW HOTEL is a charming, convenient, 11 room hotel located near the village of Codrington, Barbuda. It is near the airport and the beautiful Martello Beach and offers modern rooms which are fully screened and furnished with ceiling fans. Also available is a courtyard pool, bar and open dining area

JOLLY HARBOUR BEACH RESORT

BOONS HAVEN APARTMENTS, Boons Point

ABOVE: A BILLBOARD on Anchorage Road, promoting the wide range of hotels, restaurants, sport and leisure facilities at Dickenson Bay, Runaway Bay and Sand Haven

RIGHT: PILLAR ROCK BEACH HOTEL AND CONDOMINIUMS, Hog John Bay, is a small complex of efficient apartments and one bedroom villas with a white sand beach, freshwater pool, water sports, restaurant and shop

BLUE WATERS BEACH HOTEL, Soldier's Bay, is situated on 14 acres of tropical gardens, two palm-fringed beaches, and is within easy reach of the airport and St John's. It offers 46 beachfront rooms and eight luxury villas, each complete with mini-bar, room safes and telephones. Also nightly entertainment, water sports, beach bar, tennis, pool, boutique and shuffleboard

TOP LEFT: TRADE WINDS HOTEL & APARTMENTS is positioned on a hillside overlooking Dickenson Bay. Every apartment has a private ocean view terrace, fully fitted kitchen, living area, and television. Activities available are scuba diving, wind-surfing, water-skiing, snorkelling, parasailing, tennis and horseback riding. Hotel staff can arrange fishing trips, guided tours or golf

TOP RIGHT: MARINA BAY BEACH RESORT, Dickenson Bay, offers furnished and air-conditioned studio apartments and luxury villas. The resort is protected by 24-hour security and units are also available for sale

ABOVE: STEPHENDALE HOTEL, Fort Road, offers hospitality in the form of a relaxed environment with breezy verandahs and porches and tasty local cuisine

RIGHT: CARLISLE BAY CLUB is situated off Old Road in the south of Antigua at Carlisle Bay. This new complex has all amenities and facilities. Curtain Bluff Hotel is a five minute drive away

TOP LEFT: TRADE WINDS COVE overlooks Dickenson Bay and has full self-contained facilities including swimming pool, cable television and maid service

TOP RIGHT: ISLAND INN, Anchorage Road, boasts of 10 self-contained one bedroom studios with private balcony or patio, kitchenette and ceiling fans. Cocktail lounge and executive meeting room

ABOVE: BARRYMORE HOTEL, Fort Road, set in lush tropical gardens on the outskirts of St John's with 36 air-conditioned rooms and cable television. Facilities include two bars, swimming pool, gym, games room, business centre, conference room and maid service

LEFT: CURTAIN BLUFF HOTEL beach

BELOW: Bedroom layout at **ST JAMES'S CLUB**

ABOVE: SUNSET COVE, Runaway Bay

RIGHT: BARRYMORE BEACH CLUB,
Runaway Beach, consists of a choice of self-
contained apartments and hotel rooms with
garden view. Also available are water sports,
restaurant and bar

RIGHT: SANDPIPER REEF RESORT,
The Crosbies, on Antigua's north coast

Sun, sand & sea and blue blue sky

LORD NELSON BEACH HOTEL on the north east coast provides 16 rooms in an informal relaxed atmosphere. The location is ideal for windsurfers with a variety of sailing conditions which make it a 'windsurfers paradise'

HALCYON COVE HOTEL, Dickenson Bay. Facilities include day trips, cruises, deep-sea fishing trips and most water sports including scuba diving can be arranged at this centrally located hotel. Two restaurants, four bars, an ice-cream parlour, pool, floodlit tennis courts and shops make up the package. (Inset) Halcyon's reception area

TOP LEFT: THE ADMIRAL'S INN situated at English Harbour is an historic 200 hundred year-old building which comprises 15 air-conditioned double rooms complete with private baths. There is a restaurant, full cocktail bar, complimentary use of available boats and free transportation to nearby beaches

TOP RIGHT: RAMADA RENAISSANCE ROYAL ANTIGUAN RESORT and Deep Bay

LEFT: BANANA COVE, Dian Bay, is situated on a private peninsula along Antigua's east coast and features 30 bedroom suites, complete kitchens, modern baths, large living rooms and private balconies. There is a restaurant, bar, fresh water pool and a nearby beach with windsurfing and snorkelling

ABOVE: HALCYON HEIGHTS APARTMENTS overlooking Dickenson Bay

CLUB ANTIGUA, Jolly Harbour

RAMADA RENAISSANCE ROYAL ANTIGUAN RESORT,
Deep Bay, is a luxury resort with 282 spacious rooms, including
cottages, and meeting facilities for 700. There is a pool,
watersports, scuba diving, tennis, fitness centre, casino and three
restaurants

English Harbour

MILL REEF CLUB

THE INN, English Harbour, is an historic 28-room hotel set in 10 acres of national park with elegant rooms and a white sand beach. Perched on the hillside is the Terrace Restaurant and bar where guests can enjoy spectacular views and candlelight dining. Leisure facilities include water sports, bars, restaurants, tennis and horseback riding.

BANANA COVE RESORT, Long Bay

ANTIGUA BEACHCOMBER HOTEL, Coolidge, is located less than three minutes from V. C. Bird International Airport. An ideal base for the business and stopover traveller

GALLEON BEACH CLUB, English Harbour, on the southern-most tip of Antigua, consists of cottages and suites which include spacious living rooms and fully equipped kitchens over-looking the beaches at Freeman's Bay. There are water sports, tennis, yacht and deep-sea fishing charters, beach restaurant and bar

CATAMARAN HOTEL features 16 rooms on the shores of Falmouth Harbour, next to Nelson's Dockyard and English Harbour. There are a variety of water sports and sightseeing opportunities

PINEAPPLE BEACH CLUB, Long Bay, is an All Inclusive 130-room hotel. There are two restaurants, two bars and an electronic casino

SIBONEY BEACH CLUB, Dickenson Bay, is an intimate hotel in a tropical setting. It is also the home to the award winning Coconut Grove Restaurant which serves Caribbean and European cuisine

**ABOVE: HAWKSBILL BEACH RESORT,
Five Islands**

**RIGHT: LONG BAY HOTEL, Long Bay,
has 20 waterfront rooms, a fully equipped
villa and six housekeeping cottages set on an
idylic point of land between a reef-ringed
coral-sand beach and a protected bay**

WARRI PIER RESTAURANT, Halcyon Cove Hotel, Dickenson Bay. *Seafood, Grills, International*

OBSTI'S is a favourite eating place and focal point in St John's. *Westindian, Fast Food*

TOP: BLUE WATERS HOTEL place great importance on their cuisine

ABOVE: MILLERS BY THE SEA, Dickenson Bay. *Seafood, Westindian*

FAR RIGHT: COCONUT GROVE RESTAURANT, Dickenson Bay, is recommended by Gourmet Magazine for its *Seafood*

RIGHT: BUCCANEER COVE, BAR AND VILLAS, Dickenson Bay. *Seafood, Westindian*

TOP: LE GOURMET, otherwise known as the **ISLAND CAFE,** Fort Road. *European, Caribbean*

LEFT: WARRI PIER, Dickenson Bay

ABOVE MIDDLE: FISHERMAN'S WHARF, Seafood Restaurant and Fish Market, downtown St John's. *Seafood, Westindian*

ABOVE: KENTUCKY FRIED CHICKEN on Fort Road, St John's

LE BISTRO, Hodges Bay. Open evenings only, all year round, Tue-Sun. Reservations are required. *French, International*

JAWS, over-looking Deep Bay and the Ramada Renaissance Royal Antiguan Resort. *International*

PAVILION, Pillar Rock. *Italian, Continental*

RUM SHOP, Barbuda, a chance to meet the locals

SISTER'S TARVERN bar, Browne's Avenue, for sea moss, goat water and conch water

WEST BERLIN roadside bar, downtown St John's

HUGO'S BAR, near the downtown market, St John's, serves a 'cool' Guiness

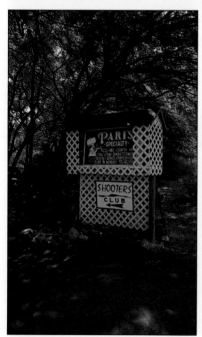

PARIS PIZZA, above Halcyon Cove
Resort. *Italian, International*

CHINA RESTAURANT, St Marys Street,
St John's

ABOVE: Local and International cuisine is prepared and presented by top chefs for a demanding clientele

RIGHT: LEMON TREE, Long Street, St John's, offers an International menu and live music

TOP LEFT: SHIRLEY HEIGHTS LOOK OUT RESTAURANT is the scene of a regular Sunday afternoon barbeque with steelband music

LEFT: ST. JAMES'S CLUB at one of their many parties

ABOVE: Fresh seafood professionally prepared and thirst quenching local juices

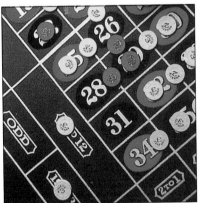

At the end of a hard day on the beach - an evening of excitement at a casino could be quite profitable!

PARADISE ENCOUNTERED

Antigua is famous for its international sailing regatta - **Sailing Week** - once a year when yachts from all over the world flock to Antigua for a week of challenging competition on the sea.

No day during this week is complete without some form of participation in the five gruelling races held every year during the last week of April. Starting off as entertainment for local yachtsmen, in 1964 British Overseas Airways Corporation (British Airways) donated a silver cup for the winner of the race between Guadeloupe and Antigua. Encouraged by this acknowledgement, the organisers decided in 1967 to hold three more days of racing in three classes: racing, cruising and traditional. Since then, **Sailing Week** has not looked back. From 1968, the number of entries multiplied with yachts from all over the world. Soon entries had to be limited to 150.

The races are a test of skill and endurance, followed avidly by hundreds of visitors, who now flock to Antigua for the event, and thousands of locals, who seize vantage points along the coast, to witness World Champion Yachts rubbing hulls with others less known but just as ambitious. While **Sailing Week** provides good fun on the sea, it is just as good an opportunity for revelry on shore. End-of-race beach parties attract sailors and spectators alike in a haze of booze, music and good fellowship. But, much of the shore activities is reserved for the last day when the daring try to walk the greasy pole with many ending up in the sea; men and women join in the nautical tug-o-war, quenching their thirst in the beer drinking competition; and the rubber raft race always produces a few sailors rendered legless by more than a few generous tots of rum.

The centre of this activity is **Nelson's Dockyard** at **English Harbour**. The dockyard is named after Admiral Lord Horatio Nelson, the British Hero of the Battle of Trafalgar during the Napoleonic wars between England and France. Nelson arrived in Antigua in 1784 at the age of 26 and stayed for three years. The house in which he lived is now a museum. He was Senior Naval Captain at the time in command of a Frigate, **Boreas**. He returned there in 1805 to provision his ship on his way to defeat Villeneuve at Trafalgar and so carve a permanent place for his name in the history books of the world.

But **English Harbour's** importance preceded Nelson - in 1725 it was selected along with Port Royal in Jamaica as one of the permanent naval

stations in the Caribbean. The development of the area was the idea of Captain Arthur Delgarno of H.M.S. South Sea Castle who argued that "English Harbour might be made a very proper place for careening and refitting, and so save HM ships the trouble of travelling to the Northern Colonies for that purpose." So grateful to Delgarno was the expatriate British community in Antigua, the Antigua Assembly voted him 200 guineas with

> "our most sincere thanks for the great benefit you have done us, in making the wharf and platform at English Harbour, a place by nature fitted, and by a law of our country appropriated, for the reception of His Majesty's ships of war, and by you, sir, rendered more safe and commodious for that purpose".

Nelson did not have a pleasant stay at **English Harbour.** A young and zealous officer, he decided to vigorously enforce the British Navigation Act which stipulated that there should be no trading between the former American colonies and the British Empire. Despite the stipulation a roaring trade was taking place between the American states and Antigua and Nevis. Nelson, not yet matured to the political realities of life, arrested ships and seized their cargo off Nevis. He also uncovered customs frauds perpetrated by merchants in St John's and the Agent Victualler in St John's. He lost no time in reporting these frauds to London. In the course of these events, he quarrelled with the Governor, General Shirley, and he was ostracised by merchants and plantation owners on Antigua.

The Antigua and Nevis merchants had considerable influence in London and they mounted an effective lobby against Nelson who was forced to drop his fraud charges. Further, year after year passed with no new appointment to a ship. Nelson began to talk of "becoming a naval mercenary in the service of the Tsar of Russia." Discussion of his "high-handed officiousness" while stationed at **English Harbour** had earned him a reputation of a trouble-maker. Five years went by before Nelson was finally recalled to naval service. Had the reputation he earned at **English Harbour** triumphed over England's need for seasoned Captains in the Napoleonic war, Nelson would have been denied his victory at the battle of Trafalgar and history might have been written rather differently.

Situated in an old Volcano cone, **English Harbour** is made up of virtually land-locked basins with only a narrow passage to the sea - this protected

Spectators seek out coastal vantage points to watch Sailing Week races

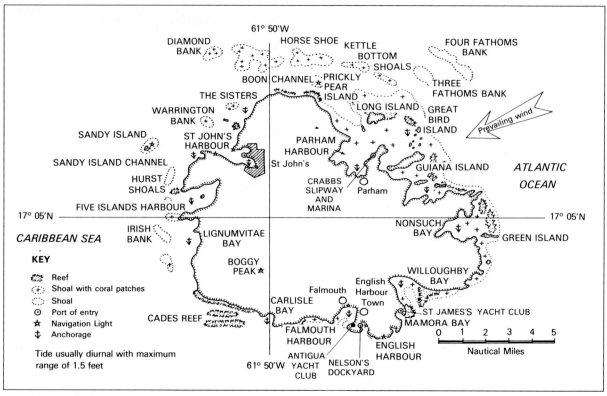

The Yachtman's Antigua

Waiting in anticipation for the start of the race

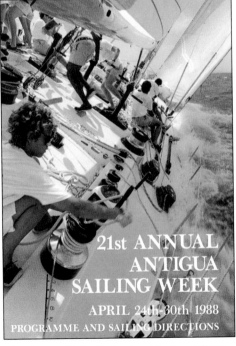

Antigua Sailing Week started off as entertainment for local yachtsmen. Today it attracts entries from all over the world. The event has its own Annual Programme and Directions

Antigua Sailing Week - Lay Day sack races and after race revellers

After race competitions allow the beautiful to put on a show, in this case, 'Kiss a Tattoo'

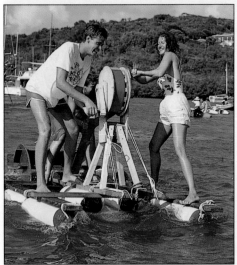

TOP: Crew members go out of their way to put matters right

ABOVE LEFT: Judges give high marks for innovation

ABOVE: Greasey Pole beats the best of them

LEFT: Non-mariners can race in any makeshift vessel

The Beer Drinking Competition is not for the timid

The Royal Antiguan Police Band beating the retreat at Nelson's Dockyard

Shirley Heights affords a spectacular sunset over Nelson's Dockyard and English Harbour

An entire section of the London docks, England, was built to receive goods, particularly sugar, from the West Indies including Antigua. This is an 18th Century painting of the West India docks in London

Shirley Heights was constructed in 1781 to give added protection to English Harbour which had become very busy

it both from the weather and from sightings from the sea. It was to defend this naturally strategic location that fortifications were built, between 1780 and 1790, on the overhanging mountain ridges by order of General Thomas Shirley when he became Captain General and Governor-in-Chief of the Leeward Islands. The ruins of those fortifications at what is now called **Shirley Heights** can still be seen today. There too is **Clarence House** - a graceful Georgian house overlooking the Dockyard. It was built in 1787 for the use of the Captain of HMS Pegasus, Prince William Henry, the Duke of Clarence, who later became King William IV of England in 1830. Later, the house was occupied by the Commissioner of the Dockyard and Governors of the island subsequently used it as a country house. Princess Margaret, the sister of Queen Elizabeth II, stayed there for a short visit on her honeymoon in 1960.

Nonetheless, the volcano cone presented great problems for human health. As a surgeon in 1808 reported:

> "more seamen die here every year than in the whole Leeward Island station besides, with the exception of Barbados. The causes of fever here are

accumulated: the men are employed at severe labour in the dockyard beneath a vertical sun: and in spite of the severest discipline find the means of procuring rum, a temptation no sailor can withstand."

The tombstones in the cemetery on **Shirley Heights** overlooking the Dockyard still tell the tale of illnesses which led many a young sailor to find a permanent resting place on Antigua.

The naval barracks and the Dockyard at **English Harbour** were abandoned by the British Admiralty in 1889. For a few years it was used as a port-of-call by the inter-colonial mail steamers, then in 1906 it was handed over to the local Government which, for lack of funds, allowed it to fall into disrepair. In May 1951, the Governor of Antigua at the time launched the Society of Friends of English Harbour to restore Nelson's Dockyard. Among the influential "friends" were Lady Churchill, the wife of Britain's former Prime Minister Winston Churchill who visited in 1961, and Prince Phillip and Princess Margaret, the husband and sister of Queen Elizabeth II.

Many of the buildings have now been restored, and the area accommodates hotels, restaurants and shops. The Dockyard, with the house in which

SHIRLEY HEIGHTS

TOP: Ruins of Officers Quarters
FAR LEFT: Powder Magazine
LEFT: The grave of Elizabeth Crofton, died 1851, from one of the many illnesses suffered by the European colonists
ABOVE: Obelisk erected in 1860, is dedicated to the 54th Regiment who lost many men due to the inhospitable conditions and environment they were forced to live in

Exterior of a distillery on Weatherell's Estate on Antigua 1823

Nelson occasionally slept during the three years he was stationed in Antigua, is spectacular, and the ruins at Shirley Heights permits the visitor to meander through naval facilities and fortifications which open an interesting vista on British naval history. At nearby Dow's Hill, the National Parks Authority maintains the **Interpretation Centre** where an audiovisual show provides a brief history of Antigua. The views of the area from Dow's Hill are breathtakingly beautiful.

Looking out from **Shirley Heights** at the panorama of **English Harbour, Falmouth Harbour** and the broad sweep inland, it is obvious how the country was shorn of its trees - the mountain sides are bare and harsh with only the hardy acacia plants holding the soil together. Throughout the countryside, apart from occasional coconut and breadfruit trees, it is the sturdy acacia with its gnarled branches and yellow blossoms that brings relief to dry and dusty plains.

But, along the coast the perfection of nature in the majestic bays and coves make up for the imperfections of man which led the sugar cane planters to destroy the forest cover of the land. The waters in **Willoughby Bay** and **Half Moon Bay, Mosquito Cove** and **Hawksbill,** run turquoise, green and blue - wondrous spectacles causing even the hardened to catch a breath.

No day is complete without seeing the Capital, **St John's**. It is congested in a friendly way. For even though most of the shops are tiny and the sidewalks are narrow, there is no feeling of pressure. Life moves on in a laid-back, relaxed atmosphere. The shops are full to overflowing with stock, and the noise of the traffic and conversations is punctuated with the rhythms pouring out of a record store or from a building where a live band may be rehearsing.

The town started around a Fort whose construction began on **Rat Island** in 1672. In 1683 the first St John's Church was built and soon the community which moved to the area grew in size. A market was built in 1702 and cross streets were laid out with broad avenues running east and west. These avenues were joined by narrower north and south cross streets. "This scheme", one expert has observed, "provided for the main facades to typically face north or south to the broad avenues."

The institutional buildings were put in place in the early 19th century: **Government House** in 1801 and a **General Post Office** in 1850. The mid 19th century was a period of great construction activity

ABOVE: Breadfruit tree

LEFT: Paw-paw fruit

TOP: Hawksbill Rock from which the Hotel Resort took its name

MIDDLE: Indian Creek, in the south of Antigua

ABOVE: View of Nelson's Harbour from Dow's Hill

CLARENCE HOUSE BUILT 1786
THIS HOUSE WAS OCCUPIED BY
KING WILLIAM IV WHEN DUKE OF
CLARENCE IN 1786/87 IT IS
NOW THE COUNTRY RESIDENCE
OF THE GOVERNOR-GENERAL OF
ANTIGUA AND BARBUDA BUT
IT IS OPEN TO VISITORS WHEN
NOT IN RESIDENCE

TOP: Clarence House, overlooking Nelson's Dockyard
ABOVE: Notice ouside Clarence House
LEFT: Interpretation Centre at Dow's Hill

Nelson's house, where he lived when he was on the island

Museum notice at Shirley Heights reads:
"The West Indian climate was not very healthy for Europeans who wore thick long clothing and at the time knew little of sanitation. However, Antigua was considered better than most islands, because of the relative dryness and the trade winds and so was used as an acclimatisation station for soldiers destined for other parts of the Caribbean. Yellow fever and malaria borne by the mosquito which bred in the cisterns were very prevalent as was dysentery and termillent fever. Rum poisoning with symptoms similar to yellow fever was also a killer as was the odd accident while drunk. It is estimated that between 1794 and 1796, 40,000 British soldiers died of disease and another 40,000 became unfit for duty. In 1804, the 70th Regiment lost 12 officers and 154 men to yellow fever. The obelisk in the cemetery is dedicated to the 54th Regiment who lost many men to yellow fever in 1850. Harriet Hipkin, 33, wife of Sgt. Major Hipkin died of the withering affects of this climate and dysentery on Jan 23rd 1851. Elizabeth Crofton, 28, wife of Philip Crofton and children, Ann and Thomas, died and was buried in the cemetery in Oct 1851."

ADMIRAL'S INN at Nelson's Dockyard, with its historic Georgian inn features, overlooks the famous English Harbour. *International, Westindian*

SHIRLEY HEIGHTS LOOKOUT RESTAURANT is an 18th Century building overlooking Nelson's Dockyard affording a panoramic view of the south coast

Falmouth Harbour

Five Islands, where HAWKSBILL BEACH RESORT is positioned, has four beaches and they are often different shades of green or turquoise simultaneously

Interior of a distillery in Antigua during the days of slavery

"In 1684, the government posted bounties of £2.10 shillings for the capture of live negroes and £1.00 for dead ones."

in St John's following a fire in 1841 which devastated many buildings. The result of different eras of construction has left the town a blend of architectural styles: Georgian, Victorian, Romantic and International.

The pedestrian in St John's faces many challenges, not least of which is the appearance and disappearance of very narrow sidewalks. This situation arises from the manner in which the town's buildings were constructed. Some buildings virtually hug the street. One resident in 1842 recorded that St John's

> "had no causeways (sidewalks) and consequently the pedestrian has to elbow his way amid trucks, handbarrows, gigs, carriages and horsemen, droves of cattle or cargoes of mules just landed from other countries, cattle carts or moving houses".

Newer buildings were forced to have sidewalks, but inevitably they are narrow and not continuous. Therefore, today the pedestrian frequently steps from sidewalk to roadside amid parked cars, moving cargo, and a constant flow of other people. But, far from being threatening, the atmosphere is exhilarating, filled with a great sense of life and healthy activity; a sense that is redoubled by the brightness of the sun's light and the warmth of its glow.

"Moving houses" are also encountered upon occasion, except that today these tiny cottages are transported by tractor and trailer, whereas in 1842 they were set on carts and pulled by oxen.

Two St John's development projects known as **Heritage Quay** and **Redcliffe Quay,** have replaced slum areas with buildings which recall the architectural form of the mid 19th century. The panoply of structures, outlined by attractive promenades, are as eye catching collectively as they are significant in their individual representation of ages past and present.

Redcliffe Quay and **Heritage Quay** are both worth visiting. Both Quays are filled with shops and restaurants, and while duty-free shopping is available in **Heritage Quay**, the shops in **Redcliffe Quay** are a virtual Aladdin's Cave of fabrics, knick-knacks, quality garments and unusual curios from the Caribbean and Latin America. **Redcliffe Quay** in particular creates the illusion of transporting the wanderer into the past. The layout of the area and the structures and architectural designs of its buildings generate a calming effect upon the spirit.

Heritage Quay may lack the West Indian

ABOVE: Cruise ships arriving at St. John's Harbour

RIGHT: HERITAGE QUAY, a modern complex of local and duty-free shops and restaurants

BOTH PAGES: The variety of shops and restaurants at HERITAGE QUAY, St John's

REDCLIFFE QUAY creates the illusion of wandering back into the past

The shop fronts of REDCLIFFE QUAY. (Inset) Old Boat Winch on Redcliffe Quay with a plaque dedicated to Dr Thomas Coke - "Father of the Methodist Missionary Society" who landed there on 25 December 1786

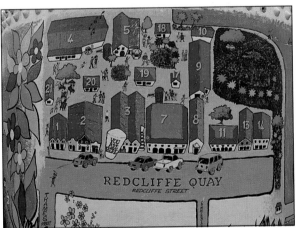

Map of Redcliffe Quay

Old red telephone box from London, England

The sights of REDCLIFFE QUAY with (above) ISLAND PHOTO proprietor/photographer Allan Aflak in Redcliffe Street

Street traders, downtown St John's

JOE MIKES'S DOWNTOWN HOTEL PLAZA offers air-conditioned rooms with TV in the hospitality room. The convenient downtown location provides easy access to the business section. Other facilities include; restaurant, ice cream parlour, lounge, casino, electronic games room, beauty salon and gift shop

Coco Shop, St Mary's Street, St John's

Buy Rite Liquor Store, St John's

The John F. Shoul Centre, Newgate Street, St John's

Food City, Deep Water Harbour, St John's

Crowded streets in the commercial areas of St John's

Emperors and Reliance Pharmacy, Redcliffe Street, St John's

Cold drinks in front of City Pharmacy, St Mary's Street, St John's

P C's Book Review, St Mary's St, St John's

The Goldsmity, Redclifffe Quay, St John's

Radio Shack at Heritage Quay, St John's

Market scene at downtown, St John's

Colourful street trader, St John's

Artist street-trading his paintings

A view of St John's from Gamble's where slaves are gathered around their primitive dwellings. In the background is the Cathedral before it was damaged by the first hurricane in 1843

ambience of **Redcliffe Quay**, but its air conditioned shops readily compensate. On a hot day, it is a welcome relief to stroll through the shops of this Quay which starts on the sea at a new deep water harbour - where cruise shops release their thousands of passengers directly into the shopping centre - and ends at the beginning of **St John's**. The quay encompasses shops of every kind - expensive jewellery, designer clothes and luggage, liquor and wines, craft and crystal. The prices are competitive with the best duty-free ports in the Caribbean, and bargains are readily available.

Antigua was an important sugar producing island in the 18th and 19th centuries, St John's has always been a busy commercial capital. **Fort James** once defended the entrance to St John's Harbour. The original fortification was built about 1675, but most of the buildings seen today were started in 1749, and the laying of the foundation was celebrated with full monastic rites. By the time of the American Revolution, there were 36 guns here, and accommodation for 70 men. In the 19th century, a gun was fired at sunrise and at sunset, and salutes were fired for visiting warships. There are ten cannons at the Fort today. They weigh about two tonnes each and can fire $1\frac{1}{2}$ miles. Twelve

men were required to handle each gun.

The **Old Court House** now accommodates a historical Museum and is well worth visiting. The building was built of freestone from Long Island, Guiana Island and Pelican Island in 1747. It was severely damaged by the great earthquake of 1843 and later restored. Besides normal court house functions, balls, dinners, bible meetings and charity sales were also held there. It was again damaged by earthquake in 1974, and reconstructed in the early 1980s.

St John's Police Station was built in 1754 on Market Street as a guard house and jail. Four years later an arsenal was added to provide a central place for the storage of munitions. It is said that the prisoners used to hold conversations with the passers-by in Newgate Street, and spread evil advice to the members of both sexes who loiter in the area. Then in 1831 the jail was moved to the barracks east of town, where it still is today. Old bayonets capping the railings of the courtyard, were placed there when the militia was disbanded in 1838. The arsenal was used up to the 1930's and Antigua's old records were kept in vaulted stone rooms that were once the cells of the jail.

Nearby is **St John's Cathedral**. As it is today,

ABOVE: View of St John's from the steps of the Cathedral

RIGHT: Fort Barrington on top of Goat's Hill

BELOW: Fort James, built in the early 18th century to protect the harbour at St John's, still affords a lovely view of the harbour. Many of its old cannons and walls are still intact and definitely worth a visit

The Old Court House, built in 1747, accommodates the Museum of Antigua & Barbuda, open Mon - Fri, 8.30am - 4.00pm, admission is free

Venezuelan Institute of Culture and Co-operation, Stapleton Lane

NOTICE
DO NOT DUMP
REFUSE HERE
OFFENDERS
WILL BE FINED
FROM
$500-$3000
BY ORDER
CBH

Polite notice

Ministry of Economic Development, Industry and Tourism

The fire brigade is always on the ready at the fire station, St John's

Police Motorcyclist in St John's

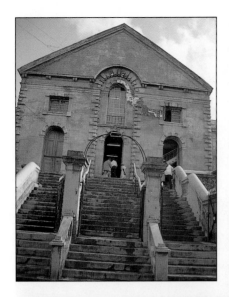

TOP LEFT: St John's Cathedral, dominating the capital

TOP RIGHT: Old bayonets cap the railings of the police station courtyard. They were placed there when the militia was disbanded in 1838

LEFT: A two tonne cannon at Fort James

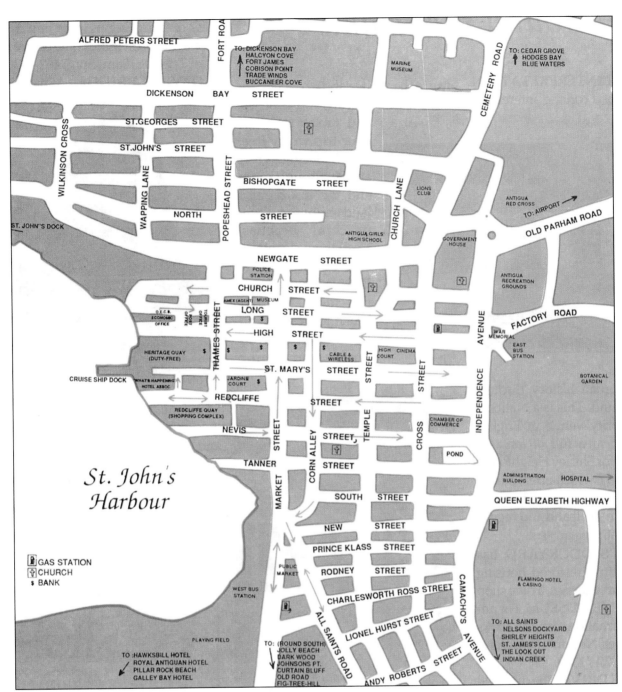

Street map of today's St John's

A panoramic view of St John's with lighthouse and Government House in foreground and a cruise ship close to Rat Island. The development and land reclaimation of the past 60 years can be seen in comparison to a similar view of St John's on pages 62-63, taken in the 1930s

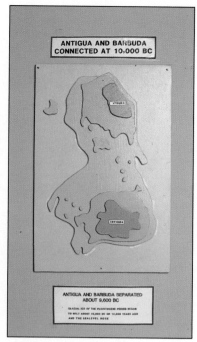

The Antigua and Barbuda Museum has a number of archeological and geological displays for the visitor

the Cathedral was built after the great earthquake of 1843 and consecrated in 1848. The first St John's Church was built in 1681, and this was replaced about 1722. It played an active part in the island's life, and was used in 1805 for the investiture of Admiral Hood by Lord Lavington. Just as pleas were being made for the church to be elevated to the status of Cathedral, the earthquake struck. The present Cathedral's interior is encased in wood in order to protect it from both hurricane and earthquake damage. This was put to good use when another earthquake struck in 1974. It is an unusual and interesting building architecturally, with two towers in a baroque style.

Not far from the Cathedral is one of the newer buildings on Antigua. Donated to the country by international businessman and philanthropist, Bruce Rappaport, and his wife Ruth, the building houses the **Antigua and Barbuda Archives** and serves as a repository for historical documents and as a display centre of the country's history.

The Prison is across the road from the Archives building. It was built in 1735 after a fund was raised to build barracks for the 38th Regiment of Foot, which was stationed in Antigua from 1707 to 1764. The present grammar school was then a hospital,

and beautiful gardens with ponds, orange groves, Turk's Head cacti and a skittle alley were situated between these two building. It was not until 1831 that the barracks was converted to its present use as a prison.

Opposite the **Prison** is the **Antigua Recreation Ground** - venue for Caribbean and international cricket and football matches. Antiguans have been able to watch two of their native sons - Vivian Richards and Richie Richardson - captain the West Indies Cricket Team to victory there. They have also seen other Antiguans like Andy Roberts, Curtley Ambrose, Kenneth Benjamin and Winston Benjamin, break into the West Indies Team through natural and graceful talent.

Sport in Antigua is pursued with an ardency that borders on religious zeal. Everywhere on the island, cricket matches will be encountered in open fields, on the beaches and on well established cricket grounds. For some, the achievement of world class status is a serious motivation. They have seen Richards, Richardson, Roberts, Ambrose and the Benjamins achieve a good living from the game. But, for most, the impetus is the pure love of cricket which Tim Hector asserts shaped "the vital character, the essential nature of the people of Antigua."

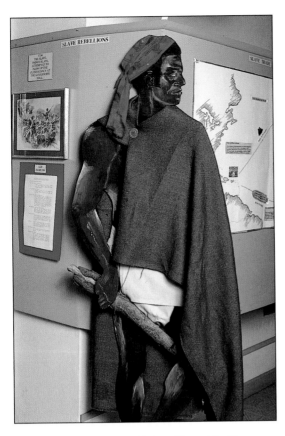

THE HISTORY OF PRINCE KLAAS
(THE PRINCE KLAAS STORY)

BORN IN 1691 IN THE GOLD COAST, CAME
TO ANTIGUA IN 1701 AS A COROMANTEE
SLAVE. KLAAS' DOMINANT SPIRIT FIERCELY
RESISTED THE CONDITION IN
WHICH HE FOUND HIMSELF. HE SIMPLY
COULD NOT ACCEPT THE ROLE OF A SLAVE,
FINDING LIFE ON THE ESTATE IRKSOME.
EVEN MORE GALLING WAS THE WHIPPING
WHICH HE HAD TO ENDURE BECAUSE HIS
PROUD AND UNBENDING SPIRIT WOULD
NOT SUBMIT TO THE WHITE MAN.
1

ABOVE: A representation of Prince Klaas at the Museum of Antigua and Barbuda. In 1736, Klaas attempted to blow up the plantocracy at the Governor's Ball

RIGHT: One of a number of plaques at the Prince Klaas Monument, St John's, which outlines part of the history of the slave leader

BELOW: Model of an Arawak village which forms a large display in the Museum in St John's

BELOW RIGHT: The Prince Klaas Monument, St John's

Cricket, the quintessential English summer sport is the number-one sport of the Caribbean. The Test record of the Westindies Cricket team is unrivalled, and they have dominated the game worldwide for the past 15 years, never having lost a series at home for 14 years. Their success is due to carefully nutured natural talent and an uninhibited approach to playing the game

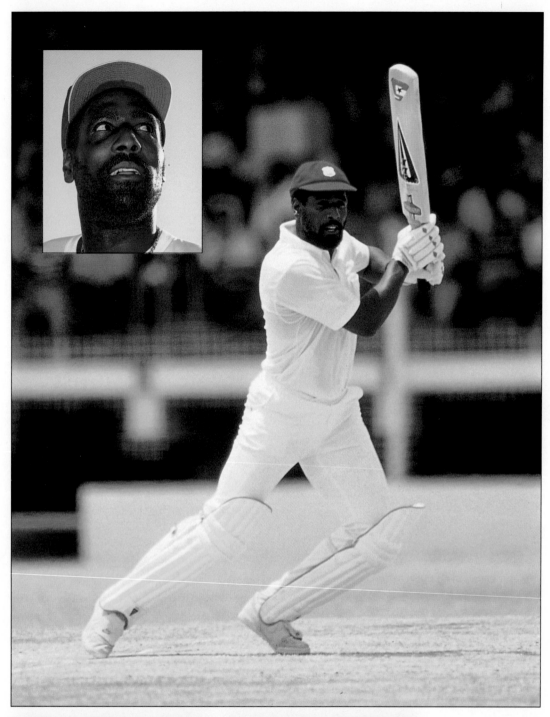

ABOVE: VIV RICHARDS, the Westindies leading run-scorer in Test Cricket and the best batsman of his generation in the world. He celebrated captaining the Westindies against England in Antigua by scoring the fastest-ever Test century - just 56 balls, in 1986

FAR LEFT: VIV RICHARDS with DR. RODNEY WILLIAMS MP, Minister for Economic Development, Industry and Tourism at the World Travel Market, London, 1993

LEFT: Vivian Richards Street in St John's

RICHIE RICHARDSON, a glorious stroke-maker and current captain of the West Indies Cricket team

CURTLEY AMBROSE, the 6 feet 8 inches fast bowler who gave up basketball to take the new ball for the Westindies. He is perhaps the best fast bowler in the world

ANDY ROBERTS helped put Antiguan cricket on the map, playing 47 Tests for Westindies between 1974 and 1984. He was the first Antiguan to play for the Westindies and with Michael Holding of Jamaica formed one of the quickest and most fearsome opening bowling attacks in Test history. (Inset) Andy Roberts is held in the highest regard on the island and has a St John's street named after him

Beach Cricket, a typical Caribbean pastime

HAMISH ANTHONY, an up and coming young cricketer from Antigua's Urlings Village, who was just 20 years old when he toured England and Australia with the Westindies in 1991

ABOVE: RICHARDSON and **RICHARDS.** Richie Richardson took over the captaincy from Viv Richards in 1991 after Richards had led Westindies for over six years. He remained unbeaten in any series during that time

RIGHT: Members of both houses of the British Parliament, along with media, arts and sports personalities who comprise the famed Lords and Commons/Celebrity Cricket Team in Antigua. The tour party under the leadership of William Cash MP, totalled 26 members and were the guests of the famous St James's Club. The group were involved in two cricket matches, one against a team picked from local Parliamentarians and other dignitaries

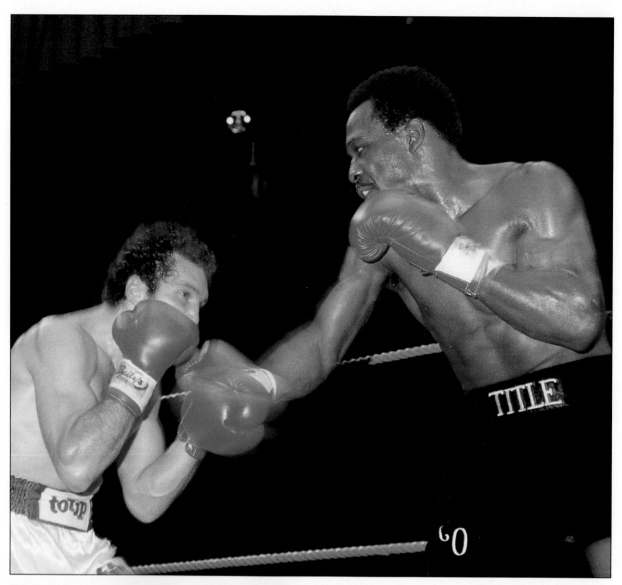

ABOVE: Antiguan born MAURICE HOPE was one of the many distinguished names who held the World Light-Middleweight belt and was indeed a very popular boxer during the early 1980s. A mixture of effervescence and an iron will to win earned him many fight fans who affectionately named him 'Mo'. Hope lived in Hackney, London, and his boxing career nearly came to an end when he damaged the retina in his right eye, but came back, with the help of ground-breaking advances in medical science and his famous determination, to become the epoch for black boxing in Britain

LEFT: *Westindian Digest* honoured Maurice Hope with its August 1980 front cover

Football ranks second in the sport played by Antiguans

Football ranks second in the sports fanaticism of Antiguans, and, like cricket, games are played in every nook and cranny of the island, although Antigua is yet to produce a world class player. Increasingly, basketball has become a popular sport with floodlit courts across the island attracting players well into the night. Great interest is also taken in Boxing although, for lack of facilities, it is not pursued in Antigua. Yet, Maurice Hope moved from Antigua to England, where training facilities are available, and rose to be the light middleweight Boxing champion of the world.

The **Antigua Recreation Ground** is home to Antigua's participation in international cricket and football matches, but it was also there that the country's first national hero, Prince Klaas, a Coromantee slave of royal birth from the Gold Coast (Ghana), who conspired to start a rebellion, was tortured and killed in 1736. He was strapped to a wheel and his bones broken one by one. It is said that he died with great fortitude. Four others were broken on the wheel, six were 'put out to dry' (hung in chains without food), and 58 were burnt at the stake, many in Otto's Pasture on the edge of St John's.

While bodies died that day the spirit which sought freedom lives on and is given expression in **Carnival** in Antigua and **Caribana** in Barbuda when the rich culture of the two islands are celebrated in a festival of music, song and dance. It is also at the **Antigua Recreation Ground** that Carnival shows and calypso contests are held. **Carnival** is always during the last week of July and the first week in August coinciding with the abolition of slavery on 1 August, 1834.

Antigua and Barbuda has a rich cultural blend of English tradition, American influence and African atavism. These have all been woven into a unique West Indian tapestry that goes beyond music, dance and art. The culture of Antiguans and Barbudans encompasses the many facets of daily life. It is recognisable in the way bowlers run up to the wicket in a game of cricket, there is almost an abandon of movement, a relaxed, jaunty hurling of the legs, a rhythm in the body language that is pure poetry; a woman simply walking down the street reflects that culture in the generous swing of her hips and the freedom of her laughter, two men talking to each other display their culture in animated gesturing with their hands and the expressive demeanour of their faces; words are never adequate in the West Indian conversation.

Football ranks second in the sports fanatacism of Antiguans and is played all over the island

Volunteers providing refreshments to the atheletes during the cycling leg of the annual Triathalon

Keep-Fit classes are springing up all over Antigua

SUPPORTING THE SPORTS MEN AND WOMEN. Local businessman, Mr Azez Hadeed of Hadeed Motors, distributors of Nissan cars on Antigua, is seen here handing over a cheque for $150,000. The Antigua and Barbuda Olympic team was jointly sponsored by Nissan/Hadeed Motors. (Left to right) The late Reuben Harris, Minister of Education and Sports; Azez Hadeed, Hadeed Motors; Rupert Lake, President Antigua and Barbuda Olympic Commitee

Take a round of golf and catch a tan - the healthy way

TOP RIGHT: Cedar Valley Golf Club

ABOVE: Halfmoon Bay Hotel Golf Course

LEFT: Woodberry Park Golf Range

World tennis super star Martina Navratilova, a regular ST JAMES'S CLUB visitor, with Debbie Davis, Antigua's Number One National Ladies Champion for the fifth year. Debbie played on Antigua's first team to be represented in the Central American and Caribbean Games, in Mexico 1990. Not only a tennis star, Debbie has a Bachelor of Science Degree in Business Administration, which she has put to professional use as manager of the St James's Club Tennis Centre since 1986

Antigua's facilities and climate are ideal for the tennis enthusiast. Many hotel courts are floodlit

Game, set and match!

Beach Volley Ball - suitable for everyone and is also one of the least expensive sports!

The Royal Antiguan Resort Netball Team plays in the Netball Business League sponsored by Antigua Masonary Products. (L to R) Lauretta Charles (Umpire), Lucia Ladoo, Joan Weekes, Delia Ephraim, Lynette James, Joy-Anne Colbourne, Deana Chatham, Ruthlyn James

The Beauticians Netball Team, St John's. (L to R) Brontella Osbourne, Cheryl-Ann Lewis, Sharline McKenzie, Janette Christopher, Deleir Octave, Cleone Parker, Joyce O'Donoghue (Coach)

Most mornings at Marina Bay, as the sun begins to rise, horses and handlers from the nearby riding school take to the sea

Horse racing at Casada Gardens Turf Club. (Inset) a gentler form of equestrianism

For a bird's eye view of the world try parasailing - you don't even have to get wet

Solo sailing is nice and easy...

Hang on in there!

CLUB ANTIGUA, Jolly Beach, is a unique and versatile All Inclusive 470 room resort, set in 40 acres of beautifully landscaped gardens bordering a superb white-sand beach. Visitors can spend a day at Club Antigua for a one-off fee which covers breakfast, lunch, dinner, drinks, all facilities and entertainment including disco. Visitors can choose either 10.00am to 6.00pm or from 2.00pm until the disco closes. Facilities include; tennis, children's club, disco, bicycles, waterskiing, windsurfing, snorkelling, sailing, four restaurants, mini casino, laundry service, bars, ice cream parlour, TV room, aerobics classes, swimming pool, shops, live entertainment and barbeque

The variety of sailing conditions around coastal Antigua and Barbuda make it a windsurfers paradise.
(Inset) The best thing to do when its calm

Fishing boats can be chartered all over the island. Here, Fishing Unlimited operate from Dickenson Bay. Its skipper, Gordon Tracey (left) and its owner, Tony Emmanuel (right) are located near Halcyon Cove Hotel. A wide choice of deep sea fishing options are available with full safety equipment and an experienced crew. (Inset) A 225lb blue marlin caught for pleasure by the crew of Rimora

More than 40 pounds of wahoo coming aboard during a deep sea fishing expedition

Fishing tournament - a record for blue marlin

An early morning fisherman near Marina Bay Resort

Water skiing is fun and quite safe. Inigo Ross of Antigua makes it look easy

Antigua's waters provide excellent conditions for all types of water sports at all levels of ability

Jolly Harbour swimming pools are up to international competition standards

Antigua and Barbuda are rich in coral reefs which attract an abundance of marine life - a scuba divers and snorkellers paradise

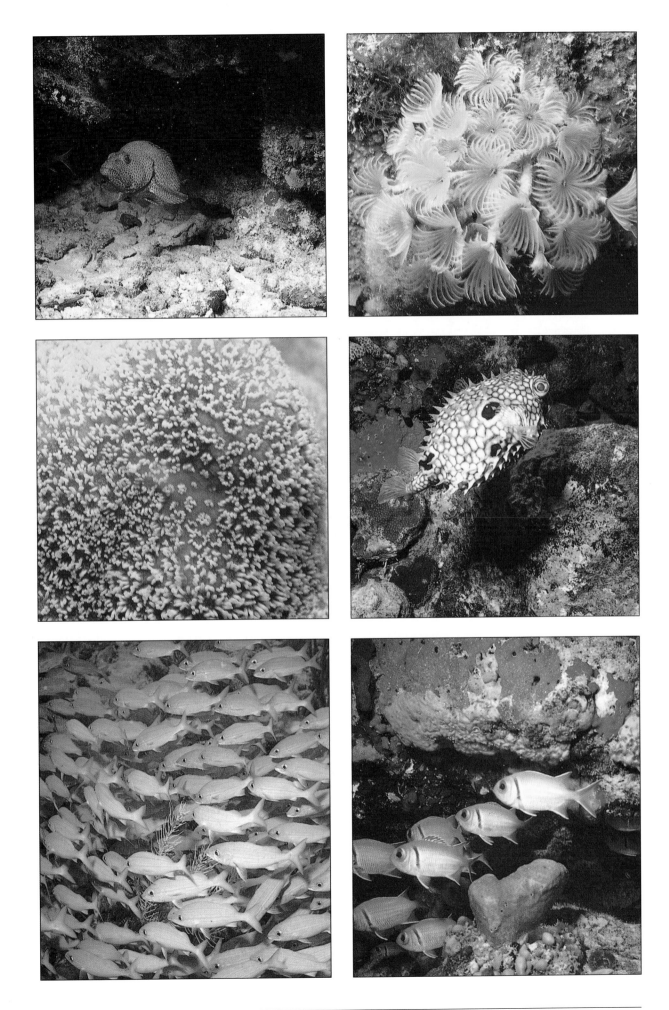

Cable & Wireless Hell's Gate Steel Orchestra setting the rhythm of Carnival

When the Africans were brought to Antigua and Barbuda, they may have been stripped of their own cultural grounding, but they did not simply adopt the culture of the coloniser wholesale. Instead, they adapted and refined it until it became peculiarly theirs. The most compelling example of this is the reverential playing of classical music on steel drums with the flair and fullness of a symphony orchestra.

Part of the culture of the country is the people's interest and awareness of events in the outside world. The ordinary man in the street will discuss the Middle East as confidently and knowledgeably as he would events in his own village. And on cricket, every Antiguan and Barbudan will hold forth with an authority born of tracing any match worth recalling.

Nowhere is the abundance of talent more prevalent, however, than in the calypso. It is the calypso competition that brings out the true spirit of the Antiguan and Barbudan personality, for the calypso performance is theatre masking serious commentary on local and international events and entertaining recitations of human relationships and behaviour. The lyrics are cleverly written, combining rhyme and rhythm with wit. No one and

nothing is safe from the scathing attention of the calypsonians who, throughout **Carnival** and **Caribana**, occupy pride of place in the hearts of the people.

The high point of **Carnival** is the selection of the Calypso King of the year. Antigua and Barbuda has produced some extremely gifted calypsonians in King Short-Shirt, King Obstinate, The Mighty Swallow, Chalice and others. The renditions of the calypsonians are quickly embraced by the steel drums and competition is intense on the selection of the calypso to be used as the "road march". This march, most inappropriately named, is a mass street "jump up" by thousands of people in extravagant costumes accompanied by vibrant steelband music and gaily decorated floats.

Culture in Antigua and Barbuda is also an amazingly unifying force, and Carnival plays a special role in that regard. At the carnival shows and in the street "jump ups", politicians and others locked in rivalry all year round drop their differences and in the spirit of camaraderie which characterises this annual festival, jump up together in the streets and actually joke with each other at bars and booths on the carnival grounds. Such are the wonders

It's all in a days fun

Calypsonian King Fiah at the Calypso King Contest

Carnival Mas Parade on stage at Antigua Recreation Ground

Carnival takes to the streets of St John's

Lord Smarty Jnr, 1993 Calypso King of Antigua

Carnival Queen Costume Competition

Village Pageant

Children at Carnival. (Inset) Young Destroyer, 1993 Junior Calypso Monarch

Majorettes on parade. (Inset) Former Calypso King, Zakari

Steel Bands set the sounds for Carnival

Carnival Mas in the colours of the national flag

Parham Church

performed by this unique cultural experience.

But what a season Carnival and Caribana bring! Music rings out everywhere throughout the periods leading up to scheduled events. By Carnival J'Ouvert morning, people from all walks of life are ready for a day of non-stop dancing through the streets, intoxicated with the driving music and the atmosphere of total abandon. There is a deliberate effort to involve children with the Children's Carnival and the Mr and Miss Teenage Pageant Contests - not that they needed encouragement, for officially involved or not, children are ready participants in the joy of life which the festivals bring.

Outside of **St John's** there are a number of interesting buildings that tell something of the history of Antigua. It is worth the trouble to see **St George's Church** in Fitches Creek. The original Chapel of Ease is believed to have been built about 1687, on land granted to Daniel Fitch. This was later transferred to the Byam family, whose family is buried there. The Church was remodelled in 1735, and has been changed very little since then. Some of the tablets date back as far as 1695. In this year a William Barnes was buried there, the first settler to be buried in a place of worship. Some of the silver in the church is very old. A planter, Lucy Blackman, left money for the purchase of silver plate in 1724.

Parham Church in the village of Parham has been described as "the finest church in the British West Indies". It was built in the 1840's after the original wooden church near Parham Hill had been burnt down. It was designed by Thomas Weeks, a famous architect, and is a beautiful and unusual design. It is a very important building, and has recently undergone considerable restoration.

Fig Tree Drive offers no buildings of special significance, but it is the most thickly wooded area of Antigua. Starting at Sweets Village, it goes through a deep defile between tall hills in the middle of the island towards **Curtain Bluff Hotel**. The height of the area combined with the overhanging trees provides a cool atmosphere set in lush, verdant surroundings. The drive takes its name from the small local bananas - figs - which grow in abundance in the area. Other fruit trees in profusion are the breadfruit, mango and tamarind. **Fig Tree Drive** provides a captivating insight into the terrain of Antigua before it was shorn of its trees and

Fig Tree Drive gives an insight into the Antiguan terrain before the introduction of sugar cane production

Swetes village

Fig Tree Drive

Codrington Airport, Barbuda

LIAT Airline fly daily from Antigua to Barbuda

vegetation in the service of sugar cane production.

A United States Naval Base and Air Force Tracking Station on Antigua is unavoidable. They command an area between **Hodges Bay** and **Coolidge** where the Airport is located. The base is inaccessible without an invitation, but many of its buildings and its very large satellite tracking station are plainly visible. The United States first gained access to this facility in 1940 when Britain granted ninety-nine year leases in exchange for fifty US destroyers. The arrangement was modified by the US-UK Mutual Defence Assistance Treaty in 1950. Since then, the Government of Antigua and Barbuda has entered sovereign arrangements with the United States Government for the continued use of the base at an annual fee. The Government uses the income from the base to service external debts.

The naval base was used by the US as part of its Sound Surveillance System (SONUS) antisubmarine programme. SONUS is reportedly "a worldwide network of fixed hydrophones that rest on the continental shelf, detect Soviet submarine movement, and send the information via satellite to the United States." The airforce tracking station is said to be utilised as part of the US space programme and is used for tracking space flights.

When the base was started in 1941, it provided better and higher paid jobs to Antiguans than were then available to them. Many were freed from the sugar plantations by securing jobs there. They also learned some technical skills that would otherwise have not been possible. While the base and the tracking station do not provide as many jobs to locals as they used to, there is obvious local regard for the role it once played. Even though the Government has been criticised from time to time by political forces outside of Antigua for allowing the United States to maintain a base there, the country continues to provide a hospitable environment for it.

Barbuda presents a special charm. Today, the island represents the nearest any one will get to seeing a West Indian island that is unspoilt. Deer and wild pig still roam freely in the scrub and theirs is the only footprint likely to be found on some beaches. Flying there is a 20 minute journey from Antigua's **V C Bird International Airport.** Landing is either at the airstrip at Codrington, the capital of Barbuda, or at the private airstrip at **Coco Point Lodge.** Apart from the magnificent beaches and crystal clear waters for swimming, lazing,

Martello Tower and Fort, Barbuda

American servicemen paying their respects at Remembrance Day ceremony

ABOVE: Game and livestock have been the mainstay of the Barbudan economy

LEFT: Redonda, inhabited only by birds. In 1993, a person claiming to be the Queen of Redonda attempted to land there but failed due to rough sea and poor weather conditions

snorkelling and scuba diving, the **Martello Tower** and Fort are very interesting. Built at the main landing place for Codrington, the tower and fort defended the southwestern approach to Barbuda and ships anchored off the landing. The tower was also used as a lookout and signal station, especially for the reporting of shipwrecks, which were a major income to the Codringtons when they leased the island. Nine guns were once placed in the embrasures. Today there is a fine view from the top, the tower being 56 feet high.

Highland House is situated on the highest point (128 feet) of Barbuda. It is believed to have been built in the 1720's and was occupied on and off by the Codrington family until 1790's. All that remains today are the ruins of a large complex that contained the main house, slave quarters, stables, offices and cisterns. However, the breathtaking view of the northern half of Barbuda is superb.

Several thousand frigate birds have found a sanctuary on Barbuda. The birds are quite majestic - their black colour is relieved by a red pouch which they inflate during nesting as a defence. Their nests are just a few feet above water, and since the birds have no fear of people they can be observed at a close distance. The approach to the sanctuary is by boat from Codrington village airport, and a visit there completes a tour of this naturally beautiful island where animals and birds still live in the wild.

There is not much on **Redonda** and it is difficult to understand why any but the extremely curious would want to go there. However, there is a man who says he is King of this volcanic rock where his only subjects are birds which, tired from flight, land upon it mostly to perform their ablutions before taking off for more beneficial places. Cedric Boston is a native of Montserrat who read law and politics at the University of Keele in England and was called to the Bar (made a Barrister) at Grays Inn. As King Cedric I, Boston says he gained the crown with the agreement of the nobles of the Court of King Juan I. This rather implausible story has actually been published in a book entitled, 'The Kingdom of Redonda, 1865-1990'.

King Juan 11 - actually the writer Jon M Wynne Tyson of Sussex, England - says that in 1865 Matthew Dowdy Shiel sailed by Redonda and bristling with the pride of recent fatherhood, claimed it as a kingdom for his son. The boy was duly brought to the island and officially proclaimed King

ABOVE: Beach at Coco Point, Barbuda

RIGHT: Spanish Point, Barbuda

Codrington Lagoon, Barbuda, home of the Frigate Bird Sanctuary located 20 minutes by boat from Codrington village. (Inset left) A fully inflated red gular pouch on a male frigate bird seeking a mate. (Inset right) Young female frigate bird distinguished by her white breast and brownish body

Phillipe 1. Upon his death, the throne was bequeathed to the poet, John Gawsworth who appointed several eminent writers such as Dylan Thomas, Ellery Queen, J B Priestly and Lawrence Durrell to various royal positions.

Gasworth became King Juan 1 passing the Kingdom to Wynne Tyson who declared himself King Juan 11. However, in February 1984 Cedric Boston claimed the Kingdom and was declared Cedric I by followers of Gawsworth on the basis that (i) they could not find

Wynne-Tyson, and (ii) since Matthew Dowdy Shiel and his son were born in Montserrat like Cedric Boston, and Montserrat's population is only 1,200 Boston and Shiel must be related, giving Boston a hereditary claim to the throne.

Despite all this, no government of Antigua and Barbuda has taken the 'Kingdom' seriously since, so far, not even the birds of Redonda have been asked to bend a knee to the royal authority of King Cedric 1 or his predecessors.

Spectacular off-shore waves break over the reef at Spanish Point, Barbuda

INVESTING IN PARADISE

I n a world of coups and crises Antigua and Barbuda is a paradise for the businessman. It has both a pleasantly tropical climate throughout the year and a long tradition of political stability based on parliamentary democracy. While the Government intervenes in the economy as a regulator in some instances, the private sector is the dominant force in the economy.

The government and the ruling Antigua Labour Party are committed to upholding the principle of free enterprise and this pledge is shared by the main political parties. Successive governments have respected the agreements and commitments made between previous administrations and investors. No investor has ever had assets nationalised or been forced to leave the island. Under the island's constitution, property can only be nationalised in exceptional circumstances and even in such cases the country's constitution demands that fair compensation must be determined by an independent authority and must be paid promptly. This constitutional requirement is unusual in developing countries and casts Antigua and Barbuda in a very attractive light for investment.

The Economy: The economy is small and open. Therefore, the country is subject to the vagaries of the economic conditions in countries from which it imports goods and services. To some extent, the effect of imported prices on the economy is moderated because the country's official currency, the Eastern Caribbean dollar, enjoys a fixed exchange rate with the US dollar (EC$2.70 = US$1.00). The Eastern Caribbean dollar which Antigua and Barbuda shares with other countries of the Leeward and Windward Islands is the strongest of the Caribbean currencies.

The external debt of the country has grown rapidly in recent years largely because of the efforts made by certain Government agencies to develop the infrastructure of the country. Tourism is the largest contributor to Gross Domestic Product. Agriculture and fisheries have dropped from 40 per cent of GDP in the 1960s to about 12 per cent. Manufacturing industries, which thrived in the decade of the 1980s, are export oriented and produce garments, paint, furniture, bedding and galvanized sheets.

Communications: The **V C Bird International Airport** comfortably accommodates the largest aircraft. Amongst the many international airlines that operate regular flights are British Airways, British West Indies Airways (BW1A), Air Canada,

BWIA was launched in 1940 and has flown the Caribbean reliably ever since. A direct London-Antigua service was introduced in July 1992

V. C. Bird International Airport can comfortably accommodate the largest aircraft

On Wednesday, 1 July, 1992, BWIA flight BW 903 landed in Antigua on the first non-stop service from London Heathrow. To commemorate the Inaugural Flight all passengers received a certificate from BWIA Senior Vice-President (UK/Europe) Bentley Roach

BWIA's new service begins. (Left to right) Yvonne Maginley, Director of Tourism; Cordell Josiah, Area Manager BWIA and Dr Rodney Williams MP, Minister of Economic Development, Industry and Tourism welcome His Excellency Mr James Thomas, United Kingdom High Commissioner for Antigua and Barbuda; Joe Esau, Chairman of BWIA and Bentley Roach, BWIA Senior Vice-President UK/Europe arriving on the inaugural BWIA non-stop London to Antigua flight

A reception held at the HAWKSBILL HOTEL, Five Islands to celebrate the historic first flight. (Left to right) Beatrix Carrington, BWIA General Sales Manager; June-Alexis Matthews, BWIA Piarco Airport, Trinidad; Bentley Roach, BWIA Senior Vice-President UK/Europe; Charles Hawley, Chairman, Antigua Hotels & Tourist Association; Esther Smith, BWIA Sales Manager, UK/Europe; Ian Burtram, former BWIA Managing Director; Cordell Josiah, BWIA Area Manager; Hon Dr Rodney Williams MP, Minister for Economic Development, Industry and Tourism; Asha Clarke, BWIA, London Heathrow; Yvonne Maginley, Director of Tourism; Tony Cowles, BWIA Sales Manager, London; His Excellency Mr James Thomas, United Kingdom High Commissioner for Antigua and Barbuda

On becoming Miss World 1993, Lisa Hanna from Jamaica, was made a special guest of Antigua's St James's Club. The whole island welcomed her with open arms

TOP LEFT: Audrey Ballantyne, Manager of the St James's Club with Lisa Hanna and Ken Ballantyne

TOP RIGHT: Arriving at V. C. Bird International Airport, with BWIA, assisted by Errol George, Aerodrome Superintendent

MIDDLE LEFT: The welcome from BWIA

MAIN PICTURE: Two Beauty Queens, Miss Antigua and Barbuda 1993, Charmine Bailey, with Lisa

BELOW: Dave Loby, Director General of Information with Lisa Hanna and her mother

ABOVE: BRITISH CALEDONIAN fly regular charter flights from the United Kingdom to Antigua

LEFT: LIAT, the Caribbean airline, is strategically based in Antigua, the hub of the Eastern Caribbean. Flights depart for numerous destinations from early morning until the sun goes down. Schedules have been arranged to allow tourists and business travellers to island-hop all over the Caribbean without having to take any luggage - and all on the same day

BOTTOM: Another flight leaves V. C. Bird International Airport

Paul Belle, (left), Commercial Accounts Manager, British Airways, Antigua, welcomes another flight. British Airways carry the greatest number of passengers to Antigua from Europe each year

A reception held at the Cadogan Square Hyatt Hotel in London after the World Travel Market, November 1993. The Antigua Tourist Board thanked those members of the United Kingdom travel trade for the success in promoting Antigua and Barbuda as a holiday and business destination, which has now taken over from the United States with the largest number of visitors. (Left to right): Dave Hamlet, Overseas Manager, Hayes and Jarvis; Marion White, Thomsons Travel; Bill McGrorty, Commercial Director of Airtours; Charles Hawley, Chair of Antigua Hotels and Tourism Association; Dr Rodney Williams MP, Minister for Economic Development, Industry and Tourism; Emma Armitage of Kuoni and John Henton of British Airways

International Travel Consultants Ltd, Thames & Church Street, St John's

BWIA Sunjet House, corner Long & Thames Street, St John's

Global Travel & Tours, High Street, St John's

Devils Bridge in north-eastern Antigua, is a natural limestone arch which produces dramatic effects of waves and sprays when the sea is running

Cruise ships arrive almost daily in St John's. Most stay all day, allowing time for passengers to take trips or just relax on a secluded beach. A view from St John's Cathedral is recommended to see how these ships dominate the capital

TOP LEFT: Sealy - bed and mattress manufacturers, Coolidge
LEFT: Lee Wind Paints, Coolidge
ABOVE: The home of Cavalier Rum at Deep Water Harbour -
one of the Caribbean's finest rums
BELOW: Deep Water Harbour and port facilities, St John's

TOP: Antigua Workers Union
BOTTOM: Diamond Estate Farm
supplies demand in the United Kingdom
FAR RIGHT: Cable & Wireless provides
international direct dialling telephone
service, telex, facsimile and data service

America Airlines, Lufthansa and the Leeward Islands Air Transport (LIAT). Geographical location makes access to the islands relatively speedy. Flying times are 2 and a half hours from Miami, 3 and a half hours from New York, 4 and a half hours from Toronto and 8 hours from London.

Located between the markets of North and South America, Antigua's port provides a sea link from Canada, the United States, Europe and the Far East. The container handling facilities at the port are modern and efficient, handling roll on, roll off and lift on, lift off cargo. Several major shipping lines call at the port providing world wide services.

Antigua and Barbuda has an excellent telecommunications service. The British company, Cable and Wireless, provides international direct dialling telephone service, as well as telex, facsimile and data service (including electronic mail and international database to Europe, North America and other parts of the Caribbean).

Industrial Relations: Despite the links between trade unions and political parties, the industrial climate of Antigua and Barbuda is remarkably harmonious. A 1975 labour code governs industrial relations and an Industrial Court settles disputes with binding decisions. There is a shortage of skilled labour, therefore the Government readily grants work permits for companies which need to import skills.

Living conditions: Those who decide to set up business in Antigua and Barbuda will enjoy a pleasant and comfortable lifestyle. Housing on the island is as good as Los Angeles or Florida in the United States or the suburbs of greater London in the United Kingdom. There are spectacular golf courses, numerous tennis courts, a squash club and, of course, hundreds of secluded beaches where a wide variety of water sports are available. Cable television on the island provides several channels of US television on a 24 hour-a-day basis. Excellent schools up to secondary education level are also available.

Financial Institutions: A number of international banks have a presence in the country, including Barclays International Ltd, Royal Bank of Canada, Bank of Nova Scotia and the Canadian Imperial Bank of Commerce. Swiss American National Bank of Antigua has the most branches in the country. There are also two locally owned banks - the Antigua Commercial Bank and the Antigua and Barbuda Investment Bank.

A number of local and international insurance companies also offer a range of insurance services.

Antigua Commercial Bank, Barbuda branch, Codrington

Swiss American Bank and Francis Trading, High Street, St John's

Antigua Commercial Bank, St Mary's & Thames Streets, St John's

Barclays Bank, High Street, St John's

Antigua Barbuda Investment Bank Ltd, High Street & Corn Alley, St John's

Canadian Imperial Bank of Commerce, High Street & Corn Alley, St John's

JOLLY HARBOUR is the largest and most modern resort complex in the Caribbean. The development includes a hotel, waterfront villas, a 144-berth marina, boat building shop, shopping centre, restaurants and a golf course. Top left shows the waterfront apartments. Of the 1800 houses currently planned, 1050 will have direct access to their own 16ft sea wall mooring

Housing improvements and positive developments in education and training are among the country's top priorities

Luxury Villas being built at the Emerald Cove Development

The State Insurance Corporation is an indigenous organisation which is capable of satisfying all local insurance needs

The Hotel Training Centre at Coolidge increases employment opportunities in the tourism industry

TOP LEFT: Price Waterhouse has been servicing clients in Antigua & Barbuda since 1973. They opened a local office in 1986

BOTTOM LEFT: Central Marketing Corporation, Kentish Road, St John's

TOP RIGHT: Medical Benefits Scheme, St John's

BOTTOM RIGHT: Growth in health care and investment in Antigua and Barbuda has been due to the stable social and economic climate of the nation

Specialised Financial Institutions: For years the country had no leasing institution. While two local finance corporations offered short-term vehicle and equipment loans, Swiss American Leasing Company - part of the Swiss American Group of Companies - now offers leasing arrangements for vehicles, office supplies and hotel furnishings.

Doing Business: There are four principal means of doing business in the country:

1. Sole Proprietorship;
2. Partnership;
3. Branch of foreign corporations;
4. Company, public or private.

No Personal Income Tax: One of the characteristics that help make Antigua and Barbuda a paradise for business is that it levies no personal income tax.

Corporation tax is imposed at a flat rate of 40 per cent on profit, double taxation treaties are in force with the United Kingdom, Canada and the USA with regard to income earned in Antigua and Barbuda.

A **property tax** at the rate of 10 percent of the annual rental value of the property is payable annually by citizens of Antigua and Barbuda. Non-

citizens pay double this rate.

The country does not impose any export duties, save for those on lobsters, sea island cotton and sugar.

Incentives for Investors: The legal basis for Antigua and Barbuda's tax holidays for investors is codified on the Fiscal Incentives Act. The length of the 'holiday' depends on the amount of value added in Antigua and Barbuda. The definition of local value added is the amount realised from the sales of the product over a continuous period of 12 months, minus:

a) Cost of imported raw materials, components, parts of components, fuels and services;
b) Wages and salaries paid to foreign nationals;
c) Profits and dividends distributed to foreign nationals;
d) Interest, management charges and other income payments to not-residents (including companies);
e) Depreciation of imports of plant, machinery and equipment.

The government offers numerous concessions to investors, particularly if the investment is substantial. Typical concessions include:

* Freedom from the payment of Corporate Tax

TOP LEFT: A variety of business signs on the Old Parham Road, St John's. BOTTOM LEFT: Island Motors and Lighthouse, Queen Elizabeth Highway, St John's. MIDDLE: Antigua & Barbuda Chamber of Commerce and Industry Ltd, Redcliffe Street, St John's. RIGHT: Man, Woman and Child sculpture outside the State Insurance Corporation building, Redcliffe Street, St John's

on the profits arising out of the profitable operations of the company for a period of 15 years in the first instance which is eligible for renewal for a further 15 years;

* Waiver of all import duties and consumption tax on the importation of materials and equipment used in the operations of the company;

* Grant of an export allowance in the form of an extended tax holiday on the exportation of goods produced in Antigua and Barbuda;

* The right to repatriate all capital royalties, dividends and profits free of all taxes or any other charges on foreign exchange transactions;

The government allows a company to import a standby electricity generator free of all import duties and consumption taxes. All office equipment and vehicles to be used in the company's operations can be imported free of duty and consumption taxes. The government grants all work permits and the necessary residential status to all expatriates who are key to a company's operations.

Off Shore Banks and Companies: In 1982, the Government introduced the International Business Corporations Act permitting off shore banking, insurance and trust corporations. The benefits of the Act include:

* full tax exemption

* no control on exchange and freedom to operate bank accounts anywhere

* no minimum capital requirement (except for (i) banking where US$1 million is required together with the filing of quarterly returns; (ii) Trusts where a minimum capital requirement of US$500,000 and the filing of quarterly returns; and (iii) Insurance companies which must file annual reports and have a reserve capital of US$250,000)

* 50 year guarantee of tax-free status

* no statutory audit required

* bearer shares permitted

The formation of an off shore company costs US$250 and is renewable every year.

Duty-free access to large markets: Tourism is the major industry in Antigua, and with 365 beaches in the country there is still plenty of scope for foreign investment. Foreign-owned hotels should have a minimum of 50 rooms. However, Antigua and Barbuda enjoys duty-free access for a number of goods into the markets of the European Community, Canada, the United States, Venezuela and eleven Caribbean countries. This access combined with the generous incentives offered by the Government recommend the country as an investors' paradise.

INFORMATION FOR INVESTORS

Price Waterhouse is one of the world's largest international organisations of accountants and consultants. Founded in 1849, it now consists of a network of 26 firms with more than 46,000 men and women in over 500 offices in 112 countries and territories. Price Waterhouse has been serving Antigua since 1973, establishing a local office in 1986.

'Doing Business in Antigua' is the most comprehensive guide to anyone investing or considering investing in Antigua and Barbuda. Below is a quick guide of what is covered in this publication.

Investor considerations
* English speaking.
* Stable government.
* Good communications.
* Development potential.
* Currency tied to US Dollar.

Business environment
* Private sector predominates.
* Generous incentives for economic development.
* Good labour relations.
* Membership in trade blocs.
* Tourism of primary importance.
* Growing financial services industry.

Foreign investment and trade opportunities
* Tax holidays and ready repatriation of capital and profits.
* Positive attitude of local persons and businesses.
* Preferential trade agreements.
* Good international communications.

Investment incentives
* A tax holiday of 5 to 15 years is available, with a 5-year extension under certain circumstances.
* Companies incorporated under the international Business Corporations Act 1982 enjoy a wide variety of incentives.
* Export-oriented businesses are eligible for tax rebates.
* Relief is given from customs duties and other indirect taxes.
* Exemption from exchange control regulations is possible.
* A guaranteed number of work permits are provided for foreign nationals.
* Trade bloc memberships include: Caricom, Lome Convention, CBI, and Caribcan.

Restrictions on foreign investment and investors
* Capital and earnings can be repatriated.
* Hundred per cent foreign ownership is permitted.
* A wide range of enterprises is available for investment.
* Joint ventures with local persons are encouraged but are not essential.
* An exchange levy of 1 per cent is charged on outward movements of currency unless exemption has been given.
* Local borrowings by a foreigner are subject to a 3 per cent stamp tax unless exemption has been given.
* Land purchases require an alien landholders' license.

Regulatory environment
* Price controls are imposed on staple goods.
* Licences are required for certain operations.
* Most goods may be freely imported under an open general license.

Banking and finance
* Full commercial banking services are available from international banks.
* Centre for offshore financial services, including banking, insurance and trust operations.
* Exchange Control approval is required for local borrowing by noncitizens.

Exporting to Antigua and Barbuda - tips for exporters
* Few restrictions are imposed on imports.
* Customs duty exemption is available for new hotels and approved industries.
* The services of a local agent are desirable to obtain speedy customs clearance.

Business entities
A locally incorporated company in Antigua is the most common vehicle for foreign investment, and often this is the most tax-efficient method. A branch of a foreign corporation can cause tax problems in the home territory.

Capital requirements
The minimum share capital is EC$2. There is no maximum.

Founder's requirements
Two subscribers are required to form a private company; a public company requires five. Company formation is a very simple matter, requiring the drafting of a

memorandum and articles of association and filing these with the Registrar of Companies. The cost is approximately EC$1,000 (US$370).

Foreign ownership/Participation in Management

Once approval for the project has been obtained, a foreigner may be a director. Employees may serve as directors at the discretion of the shareholders.

Repatriation of funds

Normally consent would be obtained from the outset. Provided any relevant taxes have been paid, Exchange Control approval will be given to remit profits in normal circumstances.

Liquidating an investment

This involves the appointment of a liquidator, who would normally be an accountant or lawyer, to wind up the company's affairs. If a company owned land and a noncitizen wished to buy, an alien landholder's license would be needed.

Tax considerations

Companies pay tax at 40 per cent of profits. All other businesses pay at a rate of 25 per cent except professionals. Companies and businesses can deduct justifiable directors' fees and proprietors' salaries in arriving at a taxable profit.

The tax advantage of the local company is that if a tax holiday is given, profits may be accumulated and not necessarily taxed in the country in which the foreign

shareholders reside until distributed as dividends. This is not always the case, of course, and depends on the tax laws of the country concerned.

Professional advice

It is essential to discuss the matter in detail and in advance with the investors' own tax advisers and with local tax advisers to ensure a tax-efficient structure.

Labour relations and social security

* All levels of staff are available locally, but skilled labour is not plentiful.
* Employer-employee relations are simplified by the Labour Code and the Industrial Court Act.
* Social security and medical benefit schemes are in operation, but there are no unemployment benefits.

Tax system

* The bulk of government revenue comes from indirect taxation.
* Resident individuals are not assessable to a personal income tax.
* Capital gains not subject to taxation.
* Tax incentives are available.

Taxation of corporations

* Dividends from resident companies are not subject to withholding tax.
* Capital gains are not subject to taxation.
* Withholding taxes are levied on certain overseas payments, including management fees.
* Restriction is placed on losses available for carryforward.

* A wide range of industries qualify for tax concessions.
* Tax holidays of up to 15 years (with five-year extension possible) are available for qualifying business.
* International business corporations (as defined) may be exempt from local taxation for 50 years.

Taxation of individuals

* Resident individuals are not subject to tax in Antigua on income from employment.
* Basically, residents have their permanent place of abode in Antigua or are present in Antigua for 183 days in a year.
* If expatriates arrive late in a tax year but are resident in the following year, they qualify as resident in the year in which they arrive. The same rule applies when they leave.

'Doing Business in Antigua and Barbuda' is an information guide published in 1991 by Price Waterhouse

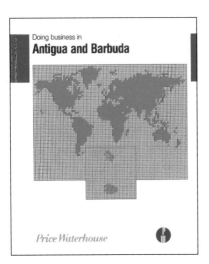

Doing business in
Antigua and Barbuda

Price Waterhouse

Morning 'till Night

From the crack of dawn, the ever present sun reaches into every nook and cranny of house and hotel waking up sleepy eyes.

But, in the rural areas of Antigua, farmers are up before the sun to prepare a meal before heading to their land. These folk are the salt of the earth, their bodies aged but lean and strong from years of toil, they are god fearing: gentle despite their strength, mannerly and correct despite their ruggedness.

Many of them have only small subsistence plots from which, year after year, they have produced crops for sale in the market place or to the Government Marketing Corporation. Their enemies do not exist among men; their foes are pests which threaten their plants and rains which seldom come. Some of them rear cattle and, day after day, armed with a prodding stick and wearing a wide straw hat to shade their heads from the sun, they walk the land, leading a herd of goats or cows, looking for good grazing ground.

For the most part, these are older people who have worked to educate their children and, in doing so, have lost the majority of them from the land. These same children, now grown up, work in offices and hotels. They too rise before the sun to catch the buses which leave the countryside early in the morning to bring passengers to central points in St John's from which they disperse to work. The bus ride is an animated affair - in a community so small, few are strangers and the journey is filled with excited conversation and laughter. Occasionally, there is a quarrel, but even this is a kind of theatre: seldom going beyond the point of loud voices, the body language of threat and counter threat - so naturally expressed - could have been choreographed for the stage. Fellow passengers, like any good audience, fully enjoy a spectacle they know will go no further than histrionics.

No morning is a morning to lie in bed - not even for the holiday maker. The greater luxury is to bask on the beach, enjoying the contrasting sensations of warming sunshine and cooling breeze. But first breakfast... breakfast in all combinations - American, European and West Indian: eggs and bacon, croissant and danish or salted fish. And what delicious fruits - pineapple, papaw and guava which were here before Columbus; bananas and oranges brought to the Caribbean by the Spanish; mango

brought from West Africa by the British.

The ultimate luxury in life is to have breakfast against the backdrop of the Caribbean sea - as blue as all the songs say it is - listening to waves as they amble up to the shore and gently splash across the hardened sand.

Beach activity is a dazzle of colour in a combination of busy jet skis, catamarans, yachts and billowing sails. Alongside this are vendors, mostly women - some short and buxom, others tall and thin, occasionally a few both tall and buxom. Their summons to buy their wares - colourful dresses, T-shirts, beads, costume jewellery made of local material - are friendly and challenging. The beach bar opens early doing a brisk business in fruit punches for kids and the faint of heart: doing better trade in rum punches for the brave.

The sea has distinctive attraction, best appreciated by snorkelling. The water over the reefs is crystal clear and reveal a colourful marine life with parrot fish, puffers, moray eel and trumpet fish darting this way and that. Deep sea diving, of course, provides a better view of the rich marine life under the sea. Keen fishermen will also find a variety of fish such as Snapper, Grouper, Wahoo, Kingfish and Lobsters which abound in the waters between Antigua and Barbuda.

As the sun finally sets on these islands bringing another day to an end and relinquishing its hold to the night, the yachts come home to dock, the beaches give up their guests to the restaurants and nightclubs, offices and factories release their workers to nocturnal pursuits. A cool atmosphere descends upon the islands as the sun disappears beyond the sea's horizon.

It is the Caribbean moon that now claims dominion, casting a romanic light across the land and onto the waters of the Caribbean and Atlantic.

Restaurants offering a wide cuisine welcome guests to candlelight and serenading minstrels. The nightclubs start much later and carry on until the small hours of the morning. The bars serve drinks to local and visitors alike. For the adventurous, moonlight cruises on a cool Caribbean sea are also available.

The day has been filled with activity. The night has wound it down gently and a taste has been shared of the 'little bit of paradise' that is Antigua and Barbuda.

THE FACE OF PARADISE

Sasha Stewart Young was the first child born in Antigua and Barbuda after midnight on the first day of Independence, November 1, 1981. Sasha, who attends Christ the King High School for Girls, is pictured with her mother, father and brother Justin. Already drawing and designing clothes, Sasha has set her sights on becoming a fashion designer. Among her favourite pastimes are ballet, tennis, playing the recorder and listening to pop star Celine Deon. Asked what she thinks is important in Antigua and Barbuda, Sasha said: "Tourism is the most important thing for Antigua and Barbuda."

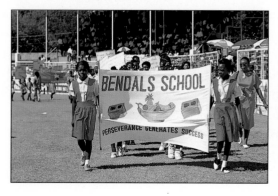

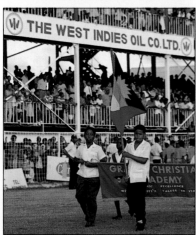

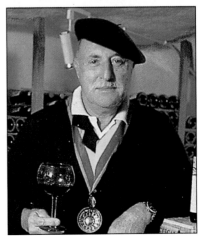

DER AUFGANG DER SONNE

Gleich einem Feuerball, blutorange, erscheint die Sonne zunehmend am Horizont der karibischen See. Ihre Strahlen, einige gelblich, andere rot, andere wiederum blendend weiß, erstrecken sich über das Wasser, verweilen tänzelnd auf dem höchsten Punkt der zarten Wellen auf ihrer Reise an die bis jetzt noch von letzten nächtlichen Schatten umhüllte Küste, deren weiße bis goldfarbenen Strände bereits von diesem morgendlichen Licht erfaßt sind. Es ist Tagesanbruch auf Antigua und Barbuda... und jeder Tag ist ein Sommertag.

So wie die Sonne weiter aufgeht, jetzt kühn und wagemutig - sie ist wie der Tag völlig erwacht - verschwindet der goldene Schimmer zunehmend und geht in einen atemberaubenden Glanz über, der sowohl das Meer als auch die Insel erobert. Die Luft ist immer noch morgendlich frisch, obwohl die Sonne bereits ihre Herrschaftsansprüche über die Erde geltend macht. Die von ihr ausgehende Wärme ist jung und noch nicht stark genug, um den nordöstlichen Wind, der stetig über das Meer streift und ihrer Hitze Einhalt gebietet, zu brechen.

Nach alter Tradition wiegen sich kleine Fischerboote auf den Wellen auf ihrem Weg zurück zur Küste, beladen mit Fischen für den Markt am Morgen. Die Fischer fuhren nachts zuvor aufs Meer mit der Gewißheit, daß der Tagesanbruch Fische an die Meeresoberfläche lockt, um gleich einem täglichen Ritus das helle Leuchten der neu geborenen Sonne willkommen zu heißen, bevor ihre Hitze sie zwingt, kühleres Wasser in der Nähe des Meeresbodens aufzusuchen. Das rhythmische Tuckern der kleinen Außenbordmotore der Boote vermischt sich mit dem lauteren Brummen der größeren Motoren von Jet-Skis, Motorbooten und Yachten. Währenddessen beginnen diejenigen, die für das Wohl und die Zufriedenheit der Touristen sorgen, ihre Ausrüstung für die Personen zu richten, die angstvoll darauf bedacht sind, das Beste aus ihrem Aufenthalt in der Karibik zu machen.

Langsam füllt sich der Strand. Zuerst, junge Eingeborene von Antigua und Barbuda - ihre Körper strotzen vor Gesundheit - durchtrainiert und muskulös laufen sie den Strand entlang und tauchen gelegentlich ins Wasser, um sich von dessen belebender Kraft erfrischen zu lassen. Auch Touristen erscheinen zu dieser morgendlich glanzvollen Stunde und geben sich sehnsuchtsvoll den Wellen des Meeres hin, strecken sich aus, lockern ihre Muskeln, bauen innere

Spannungen ab und wenden ihr Gesicht der Sonne zu und genießen das prickelnde Gefühl der Berührung herrlicher Sonnenstrahlen.

Auch Vögel gehören zu diesem frühen Treibens. Es gibt 140 Arten auf Antigua und Barbuda, 90 davon sind regelmäßig zu beobachten. Einige sind Jäger - wie der braune Pelikan, der über das Meer gleitet, um plötzlich in die

Wellen zu stoßen und in genauso kurzer Zeit mit seinem morgendlichen Mahl wieder aufzutauchen. Andere flattern von Baum zu Baum in fröhlichem Gesang und tragen so zur Vollendung der Natur und ihrer Umgebung bei. Der Bananenquit und der schwarz oder graue antillische Dompfaff mit seinem roten Brustgefieder sind am häufigsten anzutreffen.

Je mehr die Sonne ihre Vorherrschaft über die Erde gewinnt, desto mehr taucht sie die Inseln in ihr Licht, und desto lebendiger werden die Farben. Die Blätter von Pflanzen sind jetzt leuchtend grün, Blumen - die exotische Bougainvillea, der Hibiskus und Oleander - sind rot, gelblich, weiß und sogar purpur. Kokusnußpalmen und andere Palmenarten, die seit Jahrzehnten majestätisch an den Küsten dieser Inseln stehen, scheinen nun die Himmelsliter hinaufzusteigen in das klare Himmelsblau, welches nur hier und dort von kleinen, zarten Wolken unterbrochen wird. Besonders alte oder junge Palmen biegen sich gelegentlich im Wind, als Reaktion auf dessen Stärke. Aber sogar dieses Sich-Vorbeugen hat ein bestimmtes Maß an Anmut, ein Reiz, der nicht einer Unterwerfung unter eine unwillkommene Kraft gleichkommt, sondern eher einer Hingabe an die Anziehungskraft der Natur entspricht.

Die Küsten - 365 Strände und kleine Buchten - sind der Anfang eines Stücks Paradies', das gleiche Paradies, welches Christoph Kolumbus im Jahre 1493 auf seiner zweiten Reise in die sogenannte 'Neue Welt' vorfand. Er sah diese Inseln und nannte sie 'Antigua' und 'Barbuda'.

GEOGRAPHIE UND VORGESCHICHTE

Antigua umfaßt 280 Quadratkilometer (108 Quadratmeilen) und Barbuda 160 Quadratkilometer (62 Quadratmeilen). Diese zwei Inseln zusammen mit Redonda (1.6 Quadratkilometer) ergeben das Gebiet von Antigua und Barbuda. Im Gegensatz zu Redonda, welches unbewohnt ist, leben auf Antigua ungefähr 85000 und auf Barbuda 1500 Menschen. Die letzte Bevölkerungszählung wurde in den siebziger Jahren durchgeführt, genauere Zahlen sind nicht erhältlich.

Diese Inseln wurden vor Christi Geburt bevölkert. Es ist erwiesen, daß Bewohner aus der mittelindianischen Zeit schon um 1775 vor Christus in Jolly Beach auf Antigua lebten. Sie sind unter dem Namen 'Siboney' (Steinmenschen) bekannt. Ungefähr 500 v. Chr. lebten Nomaden in North Sound und betrieben dort Fischfang. Die Insel blieb für lange Zeit unbewohnt. Erst 35 n. Chr. verließen Indianer des Arawak Stammes ihre Heimat in Venezuela und kamen nach Antigua und errichteten Fischerdörfer und Töpfereien in der Nähe von Indian Creek und betrieben Landwirtschaft. Um 1200 n. Chr. brach ein anderer Indianerstamm von Südamerika in die Karibik auf und erreichte Dominika und St. Kitts über die Inselketten. Diese sogenannten Caribs besiegten den Arawak Stamm auf Antigua, nahmen Frauen und Kinder als Sklaven und ermordeten die Männer. Sie nannta Antigua 'Waladli', Barbuda 'Wa'omoni' und Redonda 'Ocanamanru'.

Der größte Bevölkerungsanteil von Antigua und Barbuda ist niemals auf Redonda gewesen, eine schon immer 'verlassene, steil abfallende und furcherregende Felseninsel. Man profitierte auf verschiedene Weise von dieser Insel. Der Grat der Felsen diente zum Anbau von Maniok für Seefahrer, es werden Briefmarken für diese Insel herausgegeben und gewann Phosphate aus Vogelguano. Letzendlich aber ist und bleibt sie nur eine Zufluchtsstätte für Vögel.

Ein Mann jedoch bezeichnet Redonda als sein 'Königreich'. Jon M. Wynne Tyson von Sussex in England sagt, daß er der König dieser vulkanischen Insel sei wo seine einzigen Untertanen Vögel

seien, die sich müde vom langen Flug auf ihr niederlassen, um ihre sich zu waschen, bevor sie zu freundlicheren Gefilden aufbrechen.

Seine Ansprüche auf die Insel gehen zurück ins Jahr 1865, als Matthew Dowdy Shiell an Redonda vorbeisegelte und stolzerfüllt aufgrund der kürzlichen Geburt seines Sohnes, das Land als Königreich für diesen erklärte. Dieser Sohn wurde zur richtigen Zeit auf die Insel gebracht und offiziell zu König Phillipe I. ernannt. Nach dessen Tod wurde der Thron an den Schriftsteller und Poeten John Gawsworth vererbt, der einige angesehene Gelehrte, wie Dylan Thomas, Ellery Queen, J.B. Priestly und Lawrence Durrell mit verschiedenen königlichen Ämtern betraute. Gawsworth wurde König Juan I., nach ihm regierte Wynne Tyson als König Juan II. die Insel. Bis jetzt hat keine Regierung von Antigua und Barbuda das 'Königreich' ernst genommen, wahrscheinlich, da noch nicht einmal von den Vögeln von Rendonda verlangt wurde, sich vor Ihrer königlichen Majestät, 'König Juan II.', zu verbeugen.

EIN KURZER GESCHICHTSÜBERBLICK

Antigua wurde 1632 das erste Mal von Europäern besiedelt, als England eine Delegation von der westinischen Hauptkolonie, St. Kitts, unter der Leitung von Hauptmann Edward Warner nach Antigua entsandte, um die Insel einzunehmen. Abgesehen von einer kurzen Zeit in 1666, als sie von den Franzosen erobert wurde, blieb Antigua bis zu seiner Unabhängigkeit am 1. August 1981 in englischer Hand. Es ist bis zum heutigen Zeitpunkt eine Monarchie, die gemeinsam mit Großbritannien Königin Elisabeth II. als Staatsoberhaupt anerkennt. Barbuda war ein weiteres englisches Besitztum, wurde aber am 1. August 1860 offiziell an Antigua angegliedert.

Der Mann, der die guten Beziehungen zwischen Antigua und Barbuda herstellte, war Sir Christopher Codrington, der 1674 von Barbados nach Antigua kam und die erste große Zuckerrohrplantage anlegte. Er benannte sie nach seiner Tochter Betty, Betty's Hope. Bis in die siebziger Jahre dieses Jahrhunderts blieb die Herstellung von Zucker Antiguas Haupteinnahmequelle. Sie hinterließ jedoch eine Vielzahl von wirschaftlichen Problemen, hauptsächlich weil sie die größte Fläche der Insel in Anspruch nahm. Codrington pachtete ebenfalls Barbuda von der englischen Krone für einen jährlichem Betrag von 'einem gemästeten Schwein, falls dies gefordert werde'. Barbuda soll zu dieser Zeit angeblich Codringtons 'Zuchtstall' für 'Qualitätsslaven' gewesen sein. Es gibt jedoch diesbezüglich keine eindeutigen Beweise.

Codrington wurde durch seinen Erfolg in der Zuckerherstellung zu einem Vorbild und ermutigte andere Personen ihm gleich zu tun. Dies führte zu einer großen Ausbreitung von Zuckerplantagen auf Antigua. Die weit über die Insel verstreuten Zuckermühlen sind Zeugen dieser Vergangenheit. Mit dieser Erhöhung der Zuckerproduktion ging die Vernichtung der Vegetation von Antigua einher. Gregson

Davis sagt in seinem Werk 'Antigua Black': "Die Abholzung und völlige Einebnung des Regenwaldes war sowohl irreversibel, als auch ausgesprochen kurzsichtig". Abgesehen von dem üppig grünen Feigenwäldchen, gibt es heute bedauernswerter Weise keine Wälder auf Antigua. Die Vernichtung der Vielfalt der Natur der Insel ist jedoch nicht das einzige Resultat der mutwilligen Zerstörung der Vegetation. Dürre und Trockenheit waren die Folge, da Bäumen und Pflanzen fehlten, die die Feuchtigkeit in ihren Wurzeln speichern konnten. Die Regierung von Antigua hat versucht dem entgegenzutreten, indem sie den Potswork Damm bauen ließ, ein riesiger Stausee in der Mitte der Insel, und veranlaßte zusätzlich die Errichtung von Entsalzungs und Trinkwasseraufbereitungsanlagen für private und industrielle Zwecke.

Im Jahre 1678 bestand die Hälfte der Inselbevölkerung aus von der Westküste Afrikas stammenden, schwarzen Sklaven, die auf den Zuckerplantagen arbeiteten. Das brutale und menschenunwürdige System von Sklaverei ist kein Geheimnis. Den Sklaven auf Antigua erging es nicht anders als ihren Leidensgenossen in der Karibik und Süd- oder Nordamerika. Sie wurden geschlagen, arbeiteten von Sonnenaufgang bis Sonnenuntergang. Jegliche Art von Widerstand oder Ungehorsam wurde hart bestraft, bis hin zur Abtrennung von Gliedmaßen. Viele der Sklaven rebellierten gegen das System, und nur Musketen und Gewehre der Plantagenbesitzer zwangen sie, sich in ihr Schicksal zu fügen.

Die Sklaverei auf Antigua wurde zusammen mit der auf den Bahamas und Bermuda am 1. August 1834 abgeschafft. In allen anderen britischen Kolonien in der Karibik galt eine vierjährige Übergangsperiode, die sogenannte 'Lehrzeit', bevor die Sklaven ihre Freiheit erhielten. Der Grund für die unmittelbare Freilassung der Sklaven auf Antigua waren rein wirtschaftliche Gesichtspunkte. Die Plantagenbesitzer waren sich bewußt, daß ihre ehemaligen Sklaven nur auf ihren Zuckerrohrplantagen Arbeit finden konnten. Sie bezahlten ihnen einen geradezu lächerlichen Lohn, trugen aber nun nicht mehr die Verantwortung für Kleidung, Nahrung oder Unterkunft.

Währenddessen war Barbuda in Großbritannien in so große Vergessenheit geraten, daß die Verfasser der Gesetze zur Abschaffung der Sklaverei Barbuda in dem Dokument nicht erwähnten. Codrington betrieb weitrhin Sklaverei, auf Barbuda richtete jedoch am 2. April 1860 ein Schreiben an alle Sklaven mit der Bitte, sie sollten auf seinen Plantagen auf Antigua arbeiten, da es auf Barbuda nicht genügend Arbeit gäbe. Sie verweigerten. Am 1. August 1860 auf schriftliche Anordnung des britischen Königs, unterzeichnet auf der Isle of Wight, wurde Barbuda offiziell an Antigua angegliedert. Weder die Regierung von Antigua noch die freigelassenen Sklaven von Barbuda waren erfreut über diese Entwicklung, erstere dachte an die zusätzliche, finanzielle Belastung ihres Haushalts, letztere hatten eine Abneigung gegen Antigua, da sie glaubten, daß Antigua ein Ort der Bestrafung sei, da die ungehorsamen Sklaven unter ihnen auf diese Insel verurteilt wurden.

Auch nach der Abschaffung der Sklaverei verbesserten sich die Bedingungen für Schwarze nicht. Sie besaßen jetzt zwar den rechtlichen Status einer freien Person, waren praktisch gesehen aber immer noch an die Plantagenbesitzer gebunden, da sie weder Land ihr eigen nennen konnten, noch über genügend Geld verfügten, um unabhängig tätig zu sein. Sie wurden folglich weiterhin von den Grundbesitzern ausgebeutet.

In den vier Jahren nach ihrer Freilassung gelang es vielen ehemaligen Sklaven jedoch, trotz der erst kürzlich gewonnenen Freiheit und den Spätfolgen der grausamen Sklaverei, von mittellosen Arbeitern zu Hauseigentümern aufzusteigen. Sie errichteten 1037 Häuser in 27 Dörfern und Kleinstädten. Dies zeugt von ihrer Ausdauer und Entschlossenheit. Sie kauften Land auf Raten und bezahlten regelmäßig den erforderlichen Betrag. Nachdem sie ihren harten Arbeitstag auf den Plantagen beendet hatten, pflanzten sie Pisang, Yamswurzeln, Bananen und Ananas in ihren Gärten an und hatten sogar genug Zeit, um Blumenbeete zu hegen. Die Gestaltung dieser schönen Gärten wurde sorgfältig durchdacht. Sie können heute noch in Dörfern bewundert werden, beispielsweise in Liberta, das erste von freien Schwarzen errichtete Dorf.

Arbeitsbedingungen für Arbeiter verschlechterteten sich zunehmend. Der Höhepunkt der Wirtschaftsrezession Ende der dreißiger Jahre erforderte Veränderungen in Antigua und den verbleibenden westindischen Inseln. Eine königliche Kommission unter dem Vorsitz von Lord Moyne in diese Region und erreichte Antigua im Dezember 1938. Auf einer öffentlichen Versammlung, die am 1. Januar 1939 im Schulzimmer der anglikanischen Kirche in St. John's, der Hauptstadt Antiguas, stattfand, richtete sich Sir Walter Citrine, ein Mitglied dieser Kommission, an die Öffentlichkeit und forderte die Gründung einer Gewerkschaft zum Kampf für Arbeiterrechte.

Einer der Zuhörer war Vere Cornwall Bird, der in den Vorstand der am 16. Januar 1939 gegründeten Gewerkschaft Antiguas gewählt wurde. Diese Gewerkschaft konnte in den folgenden Jahren für sich große Erfolge hinsichtlich ihrer Ziele - Rechte und Gerechtigkeit für Arbeiter - verbuchen. 1943 wurde V.C. Bird zum Präsidenten der Gewerkschaft ernannt.

Seitdem ist Antigua ohne V.C. Bird undenkbar. Die Geschichte dieser Insel in den letzten 45 Jahren ist hauptsächlich durch ihn geprägt worden. Er wurde 1946 in das gesetzgebende Gremium gewählt und erhielt einen Sitz im Exekutivorgan. Nach langer Vorbereitung durch die Gewerkschaft, fand das allgemeine Wahlrecht bei allgemeinen Wahlen 1951 das erste Mal Anwendung. Die Gewerkschaft hatte acht Kandidaten aufgestellt und gewann acht Sitze. Im Jahre 1956 wurde das Ministerialsystem als Regierungssystem eingeführt, und erneut fielen alle Sitze in der Legislative auf die Gewerkschaft unter V.C. Bird. 1961 erschuf man das Amt des Obersten Ministers und erhöhte die Anzahl der Sitze von 8 auf 10 mit Barbuda als eigenständigen Wahlkreis - Barbuda war vor in den Aufgabenbereich von St. John gefallen. V.C. Bird wurde zum ersten Obersten Minister, und dies sollte nicht das letzte Mal gewesen sein.

Antigua beanspruchte 1967 seine Unabhängigkeit von Großbritannien, erhielt aber nur den Status eines 'Assoziierten Staates'. Der Insel wurde die Verantwortung für alle inneren, aber nur für einige äußere Angelegenheitn übertragen. V.C. Bird wurde der erste Premier. Am 1. November 1981 wurde sowohl Antigua und Barbuda ihre uneingeschränkte Unabhängigkeit zugesprochen, als auch Bird zum ersten Premierminister ernannt.

Zwischen 1967 und 1981 unterlag Antigua und Barbuda einer politischen Umwälzung, die den Einfluß der Arbeitergewerkschaft unter Bird, der Antigua Trades and Labour Union (AT&LU), schmälerte. Mitte der fünfziger Jahre wuchs die Opposition gegen Bird und die Gewerkschaft in Angestellten- und Unternehmerkreisen. Sie stellte eigene Kandidaten für die Wahlen 1956, 1961 und 1966 auf, war jedoch jedes Mal der Verlierer. 1968 endete die Solidarität und der Zusammenhalt der Arbeiterklasse - das Rückgrat für Birds Stärke.

Unzufriedene Mitglieder der AT&LU gründeten unter der Führung von George Walter, dem ehemaligen Generalsekretär dieser AT&LU, eine neue Arbeitergewerkschaft, die Antigua Workers Union (AWU). 1970 entstand mit der Unterstützung der AWU eine neue politische Partei, die Progressive Labour Movement. Diese Arbeiterbewegung gewann 1971 die allgemeinen Wahlen. George Walter wurde Premierminister. Die Legislaturperiode von Walter und seiner Regierung wurde überschattet von der Ölkrise, die sich sowohl negativ auf den Tourismus auswirkte, als auch Preise für Importe in die Höhe schnellen ließ. Die Folgen waren verheerend. Es gibt nicht viele Regierungen, besonders junge und somit unerfahrene, die eine solche Krise überstehen. Mit dem Ziel V.C. Bird und dessen Arbeiterpartei, die Antigua Labour Party (ALP), zu vernichten verabschiedeten Walter und seine Regierung zusätzlich Gesetze, die Zensuren für Presse ermöglichten und das Versammlungsrecht einschränkten. Diese Maßnahmen zu Zeiten der Wirtschaftskrise lösten starken Widerstand bei den bestehenden politischen Kräften aus. Die allgemeinen Wahlen wurden erneut von V.C Bird und der ALP gewonnen. Zum ersten Mal jedoch gab es eine Oppositon im Parlament.

Die ALP ging auch aus den Wahlen 1980 als Sieger hervor und führte Antigua und Barbuda in die Unabhängigkeit, obwohl sich eine Anzahl von führenden Verantwortlichen auf Barbuda, 'entweder für einen eigenständigen, unabhängigen Status für Barbuda oder für den Verbleib der Kolonie in britischer Hand einsetzten'. Bei den allgemeinen Wahlen 1984 fügte die ALP der Opposition wieder eine empfindliche Niederlage zu und konnte alle Sitze, die Antigua im Parlament zustanden, für sich gewinnen. Eric Burton, der als einziger von Barbuda ins Parlament einzog, stellte die Ein-Mann-Opposition. Seitdem werden Unzufriedenheiten und andere Ansichten von außerparlamentarischen Gruppierungen an die Regierung herangetragen. Die stärkste dieser Gruppierungen ist die karibische Befreiungsbewegung von Antigua (Antigua Caribbean Liberation Movement), die von Leonard 'Tim' Hector angeführt wird. Aus einer Koalition von traditionellen, politischen Kräften entstand 1986 die Vereinigte Nationale Demokratische Partei (United National Democratic Party) unter dem Vorsitz von Dr. Ivor Heath.

Als 1972 die Zuckerraffinerien geschlossen wurde, verlor die Zuckerherstellung ihre zentrale Bedeutung für die Wirtschaft von Antigua und Barbuda, und der Tourismus, der 1960 langsam begonnen hatte, boomte. Seit 1976 sind beide Inseln von ständigen Veränderungen betroffen. Der Tourismus bringt nicht nur ein konstantes, jährliches Wirtschaftswachstum, sondern fördert den Bau von neuen und großzügigeren Hotels, Restaurants, Boutiquen und schafft nicht zuletzt neue Arbeitsplätze.

3112 Zimmer stehen zum heutigen Zeitpunkt den Touristen auf Antigua und Barbuda zur Verfügung. Sie befinden sich in exklusiven Hotels wie das wunderschöne *Coco Point Lodge* auf Barbuda und das malerische *Jumbie Bay* auf Long Island bis hin zu gemütlichen Pensionen. Das *Royal Antiguan* ist das größte Hotel der Insel und vereint alle Elemente eines idyllischen Karibikaufenthaltes mit modernst ausgestatteten Konferenzräumen. Vier Hotels verfügen über hauseigene Kasinos, die den risikofreudigen Touristen auf ein Spiel Roulette oder Black Jack einladen. Alle Hoels bieten eine Vielzahl von Wassersportarten, einschließlich Wasserski, Jet-Ski und Windsurfen. Auf Anfrage veranstaltet werden Tiefseetauchen oder Hochseefischen oder kleinere Kreuzfahrten auf Yachten.

Die meisten Hotels haben eigene Tennisplätze. Antigua hat sich tatsächlich zu einem beliebten Ressort für Tennisstars aus aller Welt entwickelt, die zu der einmal im Jahr stattfindenden, sogenannten Tenniswoche hierherkommen, um ihr Können gegen Einwohner und Gäste auf die Probe zu stellen. Golf ist ebenfalls eine beliebte Sportart der Touristen. Hotels bieten ihren Gästen die Möglichkeit, auf der überaus großzügig angelegten 18-Loch-Golfanlage des *Cedar Valley Golf Clubs* zu spielen.

Nicht nur in Hotels, sondern in die Infrastruktur des Tourismus allgemein ist viel investiert worden. 67412 Touristen kamen 1977 mit dem Flugzeug nach Antigua, 1987 hatte sich diese Zahl bereits mit 159207 mehr als verdoppelt. Antigua verfügt über einen modernen Flughafen mit Direktflügen nach Frankfurt, London, New York und Toronto. Es ist außerdem das Tor zur Ostkaribik und Südamerika. Die hier ansässige Fluggesellschaft Leeward Islands Air Transport (LIAT) fliegt täglich in Richtung dieser zwei Hauptziele.

Weiterhin wurde mit Hilfe von Investoren der Hafen von St. John's modernisiert. Die Tiefe des

(Gegenüber oben)
Sonnenuntergang
in der Bucht von
Dickenson
(Unten)
Sonnenuntergang
in Codrington,
Barbuda

Hafenbeckens und zeitgemäße Liegeplätze ermöglichen, daß sowohl riesige Kontainerschiffe, als auch Luxusdampfer hier anlegen können. 1977 lag die Zahl der Kreuzfahrttouristen, die auf Antigua an Land gingen bei 35795, bis 1987 stieg sie auf 153308.

Als auf Antigua noch Zuckerrohr angepflanzt wurde, nahmen diese Zuckerrohrfelder über 90 % der Gesamtfläche der Insel ein. Der Anbau von Früchten oder Getreide wurde von den Plantagenbesitzern nicht gefördert. Es gibt somit keine Tradition einer vielfältigen Landwirtschaft in grösserem Maßstab besonders auch, da Bauern mit der immer wieder auftretenden Dürre und Trockenheit zu kämpfen hatten. Heutzutage fehlt es der Landwirtschaft nicht an Produktivität, besonders der Anbau von Gemüse gedeiht. Die Arbeit ist zwar beschwerlich, aber ein durchdachtes System von Wasserreservoiren zur Bewässerung der Felder und ein besserer Preis für landwirtschaftliche Produkte stärkt das Interesse an dieser fruchtvollen Arbeit. Die *Antigua Black*, eine kleine, aber süße Ananas, die zu einem der Nationalsymbole geworden ist und das Wappen Antiguas prägt, wird heute zusammen mit Melonen und einer Auswahl an Gemüsesorten exportiert.

Die Wirtschaft des Landes hat von einem guten Investitionsklima profitiert. Antigua und Barbuda zieht, ausgenommen sind einige Produkte, Nutzen aus dem Zugang zu zollfreien Märkten von elf weiteren Karibikstaaten, die zum Commonwealth gehören, Kanada, den Vereinigten Staaten von Amerika und der Europäischen Gemeinschaft. Verarbeitende Industrien, besonders Zweitunternehmen, genießen die Vorzüge des Wirtschaftsstandortes der Inseln, einschließlich Steuervergünstigungen, steuerfreie Urlaube und qualifizierte Arbeiter und Fachleute. Heute produzieren Antigua und Barbuda Kleidung, Betten und Matratzen, Farbe, Elektroartikel, Öfen, Kühlschränke und Möbel.

Das Ergebnis dieser Entwicklung sind bessere Arbeitsplätze für die Einwohner von Antigua und Barbuda im Tourismus, in der Landwirtschaft und Industrie. Der Lebensstandard ist folglich höher als jemals zuvor in der Geschichte des Landes. Wichtiger erscheint noch, daß immer mehr Bürger der Inseln Besitzer von erfolgreichen Unternehmen werden und so aus ihrem Geburtsland 'ein eigenes, kleines Stück Paradies errichten'...

VOM MORGEN ZUM ABEND

In aller Frühe bereits erreicht die allgegenwärtige Sonne tagein tagaus den letzten Winkel eines jeden Hauses und Hotels und weckt sanft deren Bewohner.

In den ländlichen Gebieten von Antigua sind die Bauern bereits mit der Vorbereitung ihres Frühstücks beschäftigt, bevor sie auf ihre Felder aufbrechen. Sie sind das Salz der Erde. Ihre Körper zugen nicht mehr von jugendlicher Frische, sind jedoch schlank und zäh von Jahren harter Arbeit. Sie sind gottesfürchtig, sanft trotz ihrer Stärke, wohlerzogen und gerecht trotz ihrer Rauheit.

Viele von ihnen besitzen nur ein kleines Stück Land, von dem sie jahrein jahraus ernten und die Ware auf dem Markt oder an die Genossenschaft der Regierung verkaufen. Sie haben keine Feinde unter den Menschen, ihre Widersacher sind Schädlinge, die ihre jungen Pflanzen bedrohen, und ausbleibende Niederschläge. Einige unter ihnen züchten Vieh, und jeden Tag ziehen sie, nur bewaffnet

mit einem Stock und einem weißen Strohhut auf dem Kopf gegen die Sonne, auf der Suche nach fruchtbarem Weideland mit ihrer Herde Ziegen oder Kühe über die Insel.

Die meisten dieser Bauern sind ältere Leute, die hart gearbeitet haben, um ihren Kindern eine gute Erziehung zu ermöglichen. Diese Nachkommen werden, wenn sie erwachsen sind, der Landwirtschaft den Rücken kehren und lieber in Büros und Hotels ihr Geld verdienen. Auch sie stehen vor Sonnenaufgang auf, um die Busse zu erreichen, die jeden Morgen von verschiedenen Orten in der Provinz nach St. John's fahren, um zur Arbeit zu gelangen. Die Busfahrt ist eine lustige Angelegenheit. In einer so kleinen Gemeinschaft gibt es nur wenige Fremde, und die Reise ist erfüllt mit angeregten Unterhaltungen und Gelächter. Gelegentlich kommt es zu unbedeutenden Auseinandersetzungen, aber selbst diese sind ein Teil des morgendlichen Theaterstückes. Die Körpersprache der Beteiligten, die Provokation oder Gegenreaktion ausdrückt und selten über laute, verbale Äußerungen hinausgeht, ist so natürlich, als wäre sie für eine Aufführung einstudiert worden. Die restlichen Passagiere, wie jedes gute Publikum, finden großes Gefallen an diesem Spektakel, von dem sie wissen, daß es nur Schauspielerei bleiben wird.

Nicht ein einziger Morgen reizt zum Ausschlafen - nicht einmal die Touristen. Es bereitet größeres Vergnügen, sich am Strand zu aalen und den angenehmen Konstrast von wärmenden Sonnenstrahlen und kühlendem Wind auf der Haut zu spüren. Doch zuerst kommt das Frühstück...Frühstück in allen, erdenklichen Variationen, amerikanisch, europäisch und westindisch: Eier und gebratener Speck, Croissants und Gebäck oder gesalzener Fisch und dann erst die verlockenden Früchte - Ananas, Papaya und Guave, die schon vor Kolumbus' Ankunft auf der Insel wuchsen, Bananen und Orangen, die die Spanier in die Karibik brachten, und Mango, die die Briten aus Westafrika hier einführten. Es geht nichts über ein gutes Frühstück mit der karibischen See im Hintergrund - sie ist tatsächlich so blau, wie in vielen Liedern besungen wird - und den Wellen zu lauschen, die in Richtung Küste wandern und sanft auf feuchtem Sand auslaufen.

Das fröhliche Treiben auf dem Strand gleicht unzähligen Farbschattierungen, bestehend aus dahin gleitenden Jet-skis, Katamaranen und gesetzten Segeln. Daneben gibt es Verkäufer, hauptsächlich Frauen, einige sind klein und stämmig, andere groß und schlank, gelegentlich auch groß und stämmig. Die Art und Weise, wie sie ihre Waren, farbenprächtigen Kleider, T-Shirts, Perlen, Modeschmuck aus heimischen Materialien, anpreisen, ist freundlich und verkaufsfördernd. Die Strandbar ist früh geöffnet und macht ein gutes Geschäft mit Fruchtcocktails für Kinder und halbherzigen Erwachsenen, besser ist ihr Umsatz jedoch nach dem Verkauf von Rumcocktails für Mutige.

Die meeresbiologische Vielfalt ist am besten, beim Schnorcheln zu beobachten. Das Wasser um die Korallenriffe ist kristallklar und offenbart eine atemberaubende Unterwasserwelt mit Papageifischen, Kugelfischen, Muränen und hin- und herschnellenden Trompetenfischen. Tiefseetauchen gewährt natürlich einen besseren Einblick in diese fantastische Unterwasserwelt. Mutige Taucher treffen hier auch auf den Angler, Königsfische und Hummer, die es in großer Anzahl in den Gewässern um Antigua und Barbuda gibt.

Auf diesem Meer findet einmal jährlich die Segelwoche oder *Sailing Week* statt, die abgesehen von den profesionellen Segelregatten das angesehenste Segelrennen ist. Nicht ein Tag vergeht in dieser Woche ohne Teilnahme an einem der fünf äußerst strapaziösen Rennen, die in der letzten Aprilwoche jedes Jahres ausgetragen werden. Diese Segelwoche war ehemals eine Veranstaltung für hiesige Segler. 1964 spendete die Fluggesellschaft British Overseas Airways Corporation (heute: British Airways) einen silberenen Pokal für den Sieger des Rennens zwischen Guadeloupe und Antigua.

XIII

Die Veranstalter entschieden 1967, ermutigt durch diese Anerkennung, die Rennen auf drei Tage in drei verschiedenen Bootsklassen auszuweiten: Rennboote, Freizeityachten und traditionelle Segelboote. Seitdem ist die *Sailing Week* ein immer größer werdendes Ereignis. Die Zahl der Starter im Yachtrennen aus aller Welt hat sich seit 1968 vervielfacht. Die Startplätze mußten bald darauf auf 150 begrenzt werden.

Die Rennen sind ein Test für Können und Ausdauer und werden begeistert von Hunderten von Touristen, die nur wegen dieses Ereignisses nach Antigua kommen, und von mehreren tausend Einheimischen, die Aussichtspunkte entlang der Küste einnehmen, verfolgt. Sie wollen Zeugen sein, wenn Weltmeister und weniger bekannte, aber genauso ehrgeizige Segler, sich gegenseitig den Wind aus den Segeln nehmen. Die Segelwoche bietet jedoch nicht nur Spaß auf dem Wasser, sondern auch Festivitäten auf festem Boden. Strandpartys mit Musik und literweisen Getränken ziehen Segler und Zuschauer nach den Rennen gleichernmaßen an und formen eine Gemeinschaft. Die Hauptattraktivität bleiben mit Sicherheit die Veranstaltungen des letzten Tages. Wagehalsige versuchen, über einen eingefetteten Segelmasten von einem Boot ins andere zu gelangen und fallen dabei ins Wasser, Frauen und Männer nehmen am Tauziehen im Meer teil und stillen ihren Durst im darauffolgenden Biertrinkerwettbewerb, und der eine oder andere Segler überlebt das Gummifloßrennen nur mit großzügigen Schlücken aus der Rumflasche und mit weichen Knien.

Der Ort, an dem diese Feste stattfinden, ist *Nelson's Dockyard* von English Harbour. Diese Werft ist nach Admiral Lord Horatio Nelson benannt, dem hervorragenden, britischen Strategen, der die Schlacht von Trafalgar in den Napoleonischen Kriegen gegen Frankreich für England entscheiden konnte. 1784 im Alter von 26 Jahren erreichte Nelson Antigua und blieb für drei Jahre. Das Haus, in dem er lebte, ist heute ein Museum. Er war damals oberster Kapitän einer Frigatte, der *Boreas*. Er kehrte 1805 nach Antigua zurück, um Verpflegung und Material an Bord zu nehmen, und setzte seinen Weg fort, um Villeneuve in Trafalgar zu besiegen und sicherte sich damit einen Platz in den Analen der Weltgeschichte.

English Harbour spielte bereits vor Nelson eine entscheidende Rolle. Im frühen 18. Jahrhundert wurde es neben Port Royal auf Jamaika zu einem ständigen Marinestützpunkt in der Karibik. Es liegt an einem im Meer versunkenen Vulkankegel, dessen Spitzen aus dem Wasser ragen und so kleinere Seen bilden mit nur einem engen Zugang zum offene Ozean. Es ist somit wettergeschützt und vom Meer aus nicht einzusehen.

Zu Verteidigungszwecken wurden zwischen 1780 bis 1790 Befestigungsanlagen auf den überhängenden Felsen dieses strategisch wichtigen Ortes gebaut. Den Befehl dazu gab General Thomas Shirley, als er zum obersten Befehlshaber und Gouverneur der Leeward Inseln ernannt wurde. Die Reste dieser Befestigungsanlagen, die heute *Shirley Heights* heißen, sind noch zu sehen. Dort befindet sich ebenfalls das Haus des Herzogs von Clarence, *Clarence House*, dem späteren englischen König William IV. Er bewohnte es, als er seinen Dienst in der Königlichen Marine absolvierte.

Der Blick von Shirley Heights aus auf English Harbour, Falmouth Harbour und die ausgedehnten Landschaft der Insel verdeutlicht die Folgen der Abholzung der einstigen Wälder. Die Berge sind kahl und nur karg mit Akazienbüschen bewachsen, die der Errosion entgegenstehen. Abgesehen von vereinzelten Kokusnußpalmen und Brotfruchtbäumen, ist die Akazie mit ihren knorrigen Ästen und gelben Blüten die einzige Pflanze im Inneren der Insel die etwas Abwechslung in die staubigen und trockenen Ebenen bringt.

Die Natur in ihrer Reinheit und Perfektion, die man an der Küste mit den majestätischen, größeren und kleineren Buchten vorfindet, entschädigt für die menschlichen Fehler, die dazu führten, daß Zuckerrohrpflanzer die Wälder der Insel fällten. Das Meer der *Willoughby Bay* und *Half Moon Bay*, der *Mosquito Cove* und *Hawksbill* ist türkisfarben, grünlich und blau - ein wundervolles Naturschauspiel, bei dessen Anblick der Atem eines jeden Menschen stockt.

Die Vollendung eines schönen Tages ist die Besichtigung der Hauptstadt St. John's. Sie erscheint überfüllt auf angenehme und freundliche Weise. Obwohl die meisten Läden winzig und die Gehwege schmal sind, entsteht kein Gefühl von persönlicher Enge. Das Leben läuft in ruhigen, gelassenen Bahnen. Die Geschäfte sind bis unter die Decken mit Waren gefüllt, und der Lärm des Straßenverkehrs und das Gerede der Leute scheint auf Rhythmen, die aus einem Schallplattenladen kommen, oder auf die Musik, die aus einem der Gebäude dringt und in dem eine Band möglicherweise probt, abgestimmt.

Die ersten Gebäude der Stadt wurden um ein Fort errichtet, welches 1672 auf Rat Island gebaut wurde. 1683 entstand die erste Kirche von St. John's, und bald vergrößerte sich die Gemeinde durch hinzuziehende Personen. Der Marktplatz wurde 1702 vollendet, und Straßen und Kreuzungen gebaut.

Danach kamen öffentlichen Gebäude hinzu, das Regierungshaus 1801 und 1850 ein Postgebäude. Mitte des 19. Jahrhunderts erreichte die Bautätigkeit in St. John's ihren Höhepunkt, nachdem viele Bauten dem Feuer von 1841 zu Opfer gefallen waren. Dies führte zu unterschiedlichen Konstruktionen aus verschiedenen Epochen und gab der Stadt ihre zahlreichen, architektonischen Stile - georgianische, viktorianische, internationale Architektur und Jugendstil. Mit dem St. John's-Sanierungsprojekt verschwanden kürzlich die Elendsviertel der Stadt. An ihrer Stelle wurden Gebäude errichtet, die sich an den Stil der Mitte des 19. Jahrhunderts anlehnen. Das Spektrum der Strukturen als Ganzes fällt genauso ins Auge wie ihre individuelle Gestaltung von Vergangenheit oder Gegenwart.

St. John's ist schon immer eine bedeutungsvolle Handelsstadt gewesen, da Antigua bereits im 18. und 19. Jahrhundert ein wichtiger Zuckerproduzent war. Angeblich sollen mehr als zwölf Schiffe aus London und Liverpool zu gleicher Zeit im Hafen der Insel gesehen worden sein. Die Stadt ist ein lebendiger Handelsplatz geblieben. Eine Anzahl von Banken, viele unter ihnen sind international tätig und renommiert, haben hier ihre Filialen.

St. John's bietet ebenfalls Restaurants, Einkaufsmöglichkeiten und historische Sehenswürdigkeiten. Das alte Gerichtgebäude, das sogenannte *Old Court House*, beherbergt heute ein Museum und Archiv, welches als Magazin für historische Dokumente und Anschauungsort für die Geschichte des Landes dient. Das Gebäude wurde 1747 errichtet, in dem schweren Erdbeben von 1843 beschädigt und wieder restauriert. Es erlitt erneut Schaden in einem weiteren Erdbeben 1947 und mußte ein zweites Mal aufgebaut werden. In der Nähe des Gerichtshauses befindet sich die Kathedrale von St. John's. Sie wurde an dem Ort errichtet, wo die Kirche aus dem Jahre 1683 stand, und in ihrer heutigen Form 1848 eingeweiht. Ihre zwei Türme im Barockstil dominieren das Bild der Stadt.

In nicht weiter Entfernung liegt das Freizeit- und Sportgelände von Antigua, der Austragungsort für internationale Kricket- und Fußballspiele. Die Bewohner Antiguas haben hier persönlich erlebt, wie der Manschaftsführer der Kricketmannschaft, der aus Antigua stammende Vivian Richards, das westindische Kricketteam zum Sieg führte. Sie konnten ebenfalls verfolgen, wie andere Einwohner Antiguas, Richie Richardson und Curtley Ambrose zum Beispiel, aufgrund ihrer außerordentlichen Begabung in die westindische Mannschaft aufgenommen wurden.

Antiguas Nationalheld, ein Sklave mit dem Namen *Prince Klaass* , der eine Rebellin plante , um sein Volk zu befreien, wurde gefoltert und 1736 an genau der Stelle ermordet, an der heute die Sportarena steht. An diesem Tag starb nur der Körper, der Geist und die Seele, die die Freiheit suchte,

lebt im *Carnival* auf Antigua und der *Caribana* auf Barbuda weiter, wenn die reiche Kultur von beiden Inseln in einem Festival aus Musik, Gesang und Tanz zelebriert wird.

Der Karneval auf Antigua findet immer in der letzten Woche im Juli und der ersten im August statt und fällt mit dem Jahrestag der Abschaffung der Sklaverei vom 1. August 1834 zusammen. Symbolischerweise werden die Karnevalsshows, bei denen die Kreativität der Einwohner Antiguas ihren Höhepunkt erreicht, an dem Ort ausgetragen, wo die Plantagenbesitzer versuchten, den Freiheitsdrang des Volkes zu vernichten, der in der Person von Prince Klaass verkörpert war.

Die ganze Schönheit der Einwohner von Antigua und Barbuda wird im Carnival und in der Caribana deutlich. Offensichtlich wird dies in der Art und Weise, wie sie sich geben, in ihrer gelassenen Haltung, wie sie lachen, im Rhythmus ihrer Tänze, in der unverhehlten Freude ihrer Musik und Lieder. Und da ist der Stolz in ihren Gesichtern, der über das Leiden ihrer Vorfahren unter vergangener Knechtschaft hinwegtäuscht.

Die Kostüme für die Königinnenshow sind extravagant. Deren Entwurf und Kreation beginnt bereits am Ende eines Karnevals und geht bis zur nächsten Karnevalsshow. Auf ähnliche Sorgfalt wird bei den Kostümen der Truppen geachtet, die sich auf den Straßen formieren und hinter ihren Lieblingsbands hertanzen. Der offizielle 'Marsch' wird von den Steelbands aus den gespielten und getanzten Calypsos ausgewählt.

Der Calypsowettbewerb weckt den wahren Geist eines jeden Einwohners von Antigua und Barbuda, da dessen Darbietung einem Satirestück gleichkommt und soziale, politische und wirtschaftliche Probleme in der Gesellschaft offen darlegt. Niemand und nichts ist sicher vor den wachsamen Augen der Akteure, die während des Carnival oder der Caribana den Ehrenplatz in den Herzen der Menschen einnehmen.

Und erst was für eine Zeit uns Carnival und Caribana bringen! Schon vor dem geplanten Ereignis dringt von überall her Musik. Am großen Eröffnungstag sind Personen aller Altersgruppe auf den Beinen und tanzen ohne Pausen durch die Straßen, werden mitgerissen von den Tönen der Musik und sind berauscht von der zwanglosen Atmosphäre. Es gibt Bestrebungen, Kinder offiziell in die Ausrichtung des Kinderkarnevals und des Mr-und-Miss-Teenage-Pageant-Wettbewerb, eine traditioneller Köstümerade, miteinzubeziehen. Es ist nicht so, daß sie ermutigt werden müßten, ob offiziell oder nicht, am Karneval teilzunehmen. Kinder sind bereits feste Bestandteile im Freudenstaumel, den die Festivals mit sich bringen.

Mit dem Untergang der Sonne neigt sich ein anderer Tag dem Ende zu und räumt der Nacht das Feld. Yachten finden ihren Ankerplatz, Strände verlieren ihre Gäste an Restaurants und Bars, Büros und Fabriken schließen und überlassen Menschen dem nächtlichen Treiben. Eine kühlere Brise macht sich über den Inseln breit, als die Sonne hinter dem Horizont verschwindet. Jetzt macht der karibische Mond seine Herrschaftsansprüche geltend und wirft ein romantisches Licht über das Land und das Wasser der Karibik und des Atlantiks. Restaurants für jeden Gaumen heißen Gäste zu einem Abend bei Kerzenlicht und stilvoller, musikalischer Untermalung willkommen. Diskotheken öffnen erst erheblich später und schließen in den frühen Morgenstunden. Bars bedienen Gäste und Einwohner gleichermaßen freundlich. Für Abenteuerer werden Kreuzfahrten im Mondlicht auf dem frischen, karibischen Meer angeboten.

Es war ein ereignisreicher Tag. Die Nacht hat ihm ein sanftes Ende bereitet. Ein 'kleines Stück vom Paradies' ist uns nähergebracht worden - das ist Antigua und Barbuda.

QUICK GUIDE TO ANTIGUA & BARBUDA

GETTING THERE

Antigua and Barbuda are located in the middle of the Leeward Islands in the Eastern Caribbean, approximately 17 degrees north of the equator and 1,200 miles southeast of Miami. Barbuda lies 30 miles north of Antigua.

Most visitors to Antigua arrive by air at V.C. Bird International Airport, located on the northeast corner of the island. Flights arrive daily from the US and Europe. LIAT provides scheduled services throughout the Caribbean and South America.

BY SEA

Cruise ships that visit regularly dock in Deep Water Harbour, in the capital of St. Johns. For those travelling by boat points of entry are St.John's on the west coast, English Harbour or the St James's Club on the southern shore, or Crabbs Marina on the northeast coast.

ENTRY

Proof of citizenship is required for entry - a passport, birth certificate, or voter's card is best - as well as a return or onward ticket. Upon leaving Antigua, a departure tax of $25 EC is payable if you have been in Antigua for more than a 24-hour period.

CURRENCY

The currency in Antigua and Barbuda is the Eastern Caribbean (EC) dollar, which is tied to the US dollar. Credit cards and travellers' cheques are accepted virtually everywhere (except for some small shops and restaurants), as is US currency. The exchange rate for US dollars is generally lower at hotels and restaurants than it is at banks. Normal banking hours are 8am to 1pm Monday - Thursday, and 8am to noon and 3pm to 5pm on Friday. Antours, at the corner of Long and Thames Streets, is the American Express TRS representative on the island.

CLIMATE

The temperatures range from the mid-seventies to the mid-eighties, with higher temperatures in summer, and nearly constant trade winds. Rainfall averages about 45 inches per year, so water is always precious. The rainy months are September, October and November, although a brief shower or two can happen almost any day, summer or winter.

TIME ZONE

GMT (Greenwich Mean Time) minus 4 hrs.
EST (Eastern Standard time) plus 1 hr.

ELECTRICITY

Electricity could be either 110 or 220 volt - most hotels use 110 current. Please check before using appliances.

WATER

Tap water is completely safe to drink at hotels and throughout the island bottled water is readily available.

COMMUNICATIONS

Antigua has modern telephone, telex, and cable facilities that provide 24-hour communications world-wide. AT&T has installed USA DIRECT service at the airport and a number of other locations, and Cable and Wireless can place credit card, phonecard calls, and collect calls to any location. Most hotels now have FAX facilities.

LANGUAGE

English.

POST OFFICE

The central post office is located on Long Street, St John's.

HEALTH

There are excellent physicians in Antigua and Barbuda, and there are three hospitals - two in Antigua and one in Barbuda.

SHOPPING

Store hours vary from store-to-store, most shops in St John's and the Jolly Harbour Shopping Centre are open from 9am to 5pm, Monday to Saturday. In the Heritage and Redcliffe Quay duty-free areas, many stores open on Sundays when a cruise ship is in port.

Newspapers and tourist guides are available in shops, hotels and at the airport

CHURCH SERVICES

Antigua has over 100 churches, representing Anglican, Roman Catholic, Moravian, Seventh Day Adventists, Jehovah's Witnesses, and Methodist. Information on church services is readily available at most hotels.

NATIONAL HOLIDAYS

The following is a list of national holidays; most shops, banks and governmental offices will be closed unless otherwise noted:

New Year's Day (January 1)
Good Friday
Easter Monday
Labour Day (first Monday in May)
Whit Monday
CariCom Day
(second Saturday in June)
Carnival Monday (first Monday in August)
Carnival Tuesday (the first Tuesday in August)
Independence Day (November 1)
Christmas Day (December 25)
Boxing Day (December 26)

GETTING ABOUT

BICYCLES

The more adventurous visitors should have no reservations about renting a bicycle to explore Antigua's hidden treasures. While the island's many rolling hills suggest you'll want to rent a car for your primary means of transportation, many villages, historic churchyards and secluded coves are only accessible via

A selection of travel and educational books & pamphlets available at hotels and at the book shops listed on page 300

unpaved roads, making cycling a popular alternative.

Rentals from: **Sun Cycles**, Nelson's Drive Hodges Bay, Tel: 461 0324

Take One Video & Cycle Rental, Tempo Sports, English Harbour, Tel: 460 2604

BUSES

There is no organised bus service on Antigua, at least in the conventional sense of the word. There are no numbered routes, no designated stops and no scheduled departures. Rather, individuals run their own "buses" (usually small vans), which operate sporadically from 5:30 am until nightfall. Most "routes" connect St Johns's with the outlying districts of the island. If you have no set schedule, these buses offer a clean, safe and inexpensive way to see parts of

Antigua that most visitors miss. Be sure to establish a fare in advance with the driver.

DRIVING

A temporary 90-day Antiguan driver's license is required by law and this can be easily obtained, either through the car rental agency or at a police station, by showing a valid driver's license and paying a fee. Antigua follows the British system of driving - remember to keep your vehicle to the left. Most gas stations will accept either US or EC dollars and most of the island has a posted speed limit of 40 miles per hour, except for St John's and the villages, where it is usually 20 miles per hour.

Allow plenty of time for your journeys and have no hesitation about asking local people for directions. Drivers should be careful of potholes which are common. Be sure your rental vehicle is equipped with a spare tyre and a wheel-jack in case of emergencies.

CAR RENTALS

A rental car or a four-wheel drive vehicle is undoubtedly the most popular means of getting around Antigua. There are many car rental companies from which to choose.

Avis Rent - A - Car, Powells Estate, Box 849, St John`s, Tel: 462 2840/7
Jolly Harbour Tel: 462 7688
St James`s Club Tel: 460 5000
Budget Rent-a-Car, Powells Estate, Box 1600, St John`s, Tel: 462 3009/3051
St Mary's Street, Tel: 462 3007
Capital Rental & Tours, High Street, Box

355, St John`s, Tel: 462 0836/461 2165

Carib Car Rental - Hodges Bay, Box 1528, St John`s, Tel: 462 2062

Charles Apartment & Car Rentals, Upper Gambles, Box 1055, St John`s, Tel: 461 0424/462 4452

Dion Rent-A-Car, Coolidge, Tel: 462 3466

Dollar Rent-A-Car, Nevis Street, Box 1005, St John`s, Tel: 462 0362

Heritage Quay, Tel: 462 5798

Jolly Beach, Tel: 462 7577

Gore Ivor Car Rental, Falmouth, Tel: 460 1241

Hertz Rent-A-Car, All Saints Road, Box 1323, St John's, Tel: 462 4114/5

Huntley Car Rental, Alfred Peters Street, Tel: 462 1575

Jonas Rent-A-Car, Factory Road, Box 1831, St John`s, Tel: 462 3760

Matthew's Car Rental, Sutherlands, Box 926, St John`s, Tel: 461 1776

National Car Rental, All Saints Road, Box 405, St John`s, Tel: 462 2113

Prince's Rent-A-Car & Clothing Centre, Fort Road, St John`s, Tel: 462 0766

Ramco Car Rentals, Ramco Building, Camacho Avenue, St John`s, Tel: 462 3397

Rent-A-Car Association, Coolidge, Tel: 462 4600

Richards Rent-A-Car, V.C. Bird International Airport, Tel: 462 0976

Silston Car Rental System, All Saints Road, Box 405, St John`s, Tel: 462 2113

**St John`s Car Rental**, c/o- Gary, Richards Apartment Building, Branch Avenue, Box 673, St John`s, Tel: 462 0594/461 0449

Supa Rentals, McKinnon Way, Paradise View, Tel: 462 7872

Titi Rent-A-Car, English Harbour, Tel: 460 1452/1051

United Rent-A-Car, Coolidge, Tel: 462 3021

Village Car Rental, Anchorage Road, Box 1309, St John`s. Tel: 462 3751/461 3746

TAXIS

First-time visitors to Antigua may feel more comfortable travelling by cab. Most taxis are individually owned and belong to an association that controls their rates. Hotels usually post standard rates to the popular destinations. Hailing a cab on the street (with the exception of the Heritage Quay section of St John's) is more likely to be a hit-or-miss proposition. It is easier to arrange a cab via the hotel activities desk. Negotiate the fare before you get in and be certain to establish if it is in US or EC dollars. If your trip takes you to some remote region, be sure to arrange in advance for return transportation.

SEA EXCURSIONS

Given that most of Antigua's more popular attractions are located in coastal regions, the offshore approach to transportation can add an exciting facet to your vacation plans. There are many organised sea tours, some of which include deep-sea fishing, scuba, dining and dancing. Or you can set your own agenda and pace by chartering a sloop or yacht.

CRUISES AND CHARTERS

Horatio Historic Cruises - offers a 30-minute cruise around the waters of historic Nelson's Dockyard, amidst majestic yachts and 18th-century British battlements. Tel: 460 1178

Jacal - a 25-foot Mako, offers fishing, snorkelling, or a picnic on one of Antigua's many beaches. Tel: 462 2650/461 1671

Jolly Roger Pirate Cruises - offers daily cruises with dining, dancing, various activities and an open bar. Tel: 462 2064

Legend - a 35-foot Hatteras sports fishing boat available for fishing excursions and cruises. Tel: 462 0256/0258 ext. 458.

Loafer - a 70-foot catamaran offering sailing trips to Bird Island and Prickley Pear Island. Tel: 462 2690

Lobster King - offers two different crafts, one is a 38-foot Bertram that offers half-day and full-day deep-sea fishing charters. In addition, the Lobster King Glass Bottom Boat offers a daily trip leaving from Jolly Beach at 2:30 pm for a three-hour cruise. Tel: 462 4363

Miguel`s Holiday Adventure - leaves Hodges Bay for a boat trip to Prickley Pear Island and offers an all-day picnic, snorkelling on a coral reef and fishing off the island. Tel: 461 0361

M/Y Nimrod - a 50-foot, professionally crewed fisherman, completely provisioned for deep-sea fishing charters, scuba and snorkelling trips. Tel: 464 0143

Obsession - a 45-foot Hatteras that specialises in deep-sea fishing tours, sightseeing trips and special charters in complete comfort. Tel: 462 3174

Paradise 1 - offers full-day trips or private charters, all with luncheon and open bar. Tel: 462 4158/461 9241
Quick Getaway - a 40-foot sloop available for private charters, full and half-day cruises. Tel: 462 0256/0258
Sagitoo Catamaran Cruise - offers round-the-island, sunset, moonlight, archaeological cruises and day trips. Tel: 460 1244
Sentio - a 14-metre luxury sailing ketch, caters to very small groups, families with children, honeymooners and special occasions. Tel: 464 7127
Shorty`s Glass Bottom Boat - provides spectacular views of under-water life with daily cruises departing from Miller's Bar at Halcyon Cove Hotel, Dickenson Bay.
Tito 1 - a 34-foot Scarab Supersport with twin Evinrudes, is available for day tours Tel: 460 1452/3336

TOURS
The easiest way to see Antigua is to simply join an organised sightseeing tour. Almost every hotel offers at least one, usually lasting between three and four hours.

THINGS TO DO
HEALTH & FITNESS CENTRES
BBR Sportive at Jolly Harbour offers squash, floodlit tennis courts, and a 25-metre swimming pool. Tel: 462 6260
Lotus Health Centre, at Dickenson Bay for a Swedish massage, foot reflexology or one of their stop-smoking or weight-loss programs. Tel: 462 2231
National Fitness Centre, off Old Parham Road, is a sports complex that offers weight and exercise machines, step and aerobic classes. Tel: 462 3681

Qua Sha Health Centre, Hudson Street, St John's features Chinese therapy such as massage, acupuncture, reflexology, herbal weight-loss, and special facial care. Tel: 461 6777
Temo Sports - English Harbour is a sports complex with floodlit tennis courts, glass-backed squash courts, showers and a bar/bistro. Tel: 460 1781

GOLF
Cedar Valley an 18-hole course, carts, and rental equipment. Tel: 462 0161
Halfmoon Bay - A nine-hole golf course that offers carts and a full line of equipment for rent. Tel: 460 4300

TENNIS
Second to watersports, tennis is the most popular sports activity for visitors. Most hotels provide tennis facilities and many include floodlit tennis courts. There are weekly

tournaments and competitions Nearly all hotels have residential professionals to provide hands on instruction.

HORSE BACK RIDING
Spring Hill Riding Club is located on the road to Rendezvous Bay amidst the pineapple and banana groves of Falmouth. The club offers expert tuition from their B.H.S. qualified instructor to all levels English-style riding. Tel: 460 1333 St James`s Club, Tel: 460 5000

WATER SPORTS
Halcyon Cove Hotel Watersports - offers a wide range of water sports and small boats for rent. Tel 462 0256
Offshore Sport - offers an exciting way to see Antigua and Barbuda with its selection of performance pleasure boats. Tel: 462 4886/2621
Patrick`s Windsurfing School - teaches beginners at Halcyon Cove Hotel and Lord Nelson Beach Club at Dutchman's Bay, Tel: 462 3094/0256.

SCUBA DIVING
Aquanaut Diving Centre, Box 62, St John`s, Locations:
St James`s Club Tel: 460 5000
Royal Antiguan Resort, Tel: 462 1801
Galleon Beach Club, Tel: 460 1024/1450
Dive Runaway Box 1603, St John`s, Runaway Beach Club, Tel: 462 2626
Dive Antigua, Box 251, St John`s, Halcyon Cove Hotel, Tel: 462 3483
Jolly Dive, Box 744, St John`s, Jolly Beach Hotel, Tel: 462 8305
Curtain Bluff Dive Shop, Box 288, St John`s, Curtain Bluff Hotel, Tel: 462 8400/2
Long Bay Dive Shop, Box 442, St John`s, Long Bay Hotel, Tel: 460 2005
Pirate Divers, Lord Nelson Beach Hotel, Tel: 462 3094
Dockyard Divers, Copper and Lumber Store Hotel, Tel: 464 8591, 460 1178

SIGHTS

There is lots to see in **St John's**. It is one of the oldest trading ports in the Caribbean, dating back to the early 17th Century. There are quite a few buildings over 150 years- old still in good condition and worth a visit.

Redcliffe Quay, located in lower Redcliffe Street, is a shopping complex which has been carefully restored to its original style. The oldest building in St. John's, the **Old Court House**, corner of Long and Market Streets, was constructed in 1747 from local stone. Today it houses the **Museum of Antigua and Barbuda**, which contains artefacts and displays documents tracing the history of the islands.

The Museum of Marine and Living Art, Gambles Terrace, contains an interesting collection of local seashells, samples of the numerous and distinctly different sands to be found on local beaches. Relics from old shipwrecks and photos of articles from Antigus's history.

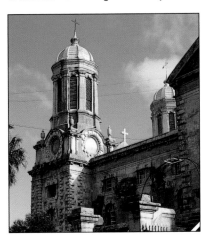

A must for all visitors is the **Anglican Cathedral of St. John the Divine,** whose twin spires dominates the capital. The original wooden structure was constructed in 1681 and replaced in 1722. In 1843, a great earthquake destroyed the church. Later that year, construction of the present stone building was started, with the consecration of the cathedral taking place in 1848. The interior of the cathedral is encased in wood to protect it against damage from hurricane and earthquakes, and indeed was tested by the quake of 1974, and again when Hurricane Hugo struck in 1989.

A quiet stroll through the cathedrals graveyard will reveal some interesting headstones, some over 300 years old.

Fort James at the northern entrance to St. John's Harbour was erected in 1675 and rebuilt in 1749. Today 10 cannons remain, each weighing over two tons. When in use these cannons were capable of shooting a cannonball two miles.

Fort Barrington, on the northern side of Deep Bay, was built on the top of **Goat Hill**, around 1779. Of all of the forts in Antigua, this fort experienced the most combative action. The present fortifications were named in honour of the British admiral who had captured St. Lucia from the French the year before. The fort, now in ruins, served as a signal station until 1960. It is easy to reach from the beach at Deep Bay.

Betty's Hope sugar plantation was established by Christopher Codrington in 1674, who named the estate for his daughter. Two large towers and the ruins of the boiling house have become an attraction and restoration of this historic site is under way.

At the end of the road to Long Bay at Indian Town Point is **Devil's Bridge**, a natural limestone arch created by the action of surf over countless years.

Harmony Hall, on the East coast near Nonsuch Bay, was built around an old sugar mill. This complex houses a restaurant & bar and an art gallery with paintings, photos, and crafts from local artists and is host to an annual crafts fair held in November.

Half Moon Bay is considered by many Antiguans to be the most beautiful beach on the island. The circular shape of the bay and its entrance facing the Atlantic combine to create a variety of surf conditions from mere ripples to crashing rollers. For those who fancy horseback riding, there's a stable near the beach.

Parham Church is the popular name for St. Peter's Anglican Church first built in around 1700. Allowed to fall into disrepair and become an eyesore, the present church was constructed in the 1840s and supervised by Thomas Weekes, a famous English architect of the mid-19th century. It has been restored and its unique octagonal shape make it one of the most distinctive and attractive churches in the Caribbean.

Close to Parham Sound is Fitches Creek, where **St George's Anglican Church** was built in 1867 and remodelled 50 years later.

Fig Tree Drive is a contrasting scenic element of this island paradise. The road from the town of Liberta to Old Road at the head of Carlisle Bay winds its way through lush vegetation and the island's rainforest. The sky often dissappears as the thick green undergrowth envelopes the twisting road.

Stop at the **Fig Tree Drive** Culture Shoppe, and apart from buying a few gifts, take a quick guided tour of the rain forest.

This route passes a number of sugar mills and many of Antigua's finest old churches.

Several old buildings are all that remains of **Fort George** ruins on Monk's Hill, where stone walls encircle the seven acre site on which the fort was built.

Falmouth Harbour has been a safe

anchorage for ships since Antigua's earliest days. It remains very much in use today, providing anchorage and facilities for modern racing sloops and motor yachts.

Fort Charles on Blake Island in Falmouth Harbour is one of the oldest forts in Antigua. Constructed in 1672, the fort once boasted 14 guns to defend Falmouth.

English Harbour is both an historic site and an active yachting centre. The British realised it was a natural haven from hurricanes and converted the harbour into a naval dockyard.

Fort Berkeley on the western entrance was built in three stages between 1704 and 1755, and served as the main defense using 29 cannons.

Nelson's Dockyard was started in 1743 and has now become a National Park. Having been carefully restored it now contains shops, quaint inns and restaurants. It is the focal point for Antigua Sailing Week.

There is a small museum housed in an elegant two-storey building known as **The Admiral's House**. This structure has been restored to serve as a hotel with a dining terrace surrounded by shading trees and stone columns.

The **Copper and Lumber Store** once provided copper sheathing for the hulls of wooden ships - today it is a hotel and restaurant.

Clarence House was built in 1787 for the use of the Duke of Clarence and later King William IV of England. It is used occasionally by the English Royal Family on special ocassions and is open to the public.

Dow's Hill Interpretation Centre provides an overview of Nelson's Dockyard - ideal to visit before exploring the dockyard. Also at Dow's Hill is the **Batcave** where according to local folklore many slaves escaped using this cave.

The high ground to the east overlooking English Harbour is referred to as **Shirley Heights**, and it includes the ruins of **Fort Shirley**. This very large fortification contains a complex called the **Royal Artillery Quarters** which houses a small museum with exhibits and maps.

Shirley Heights Lookout - is a restaurant with spectacular views of English Harbour, Nelson's Dockyard, and Falmouth Harbour. Every Sunday this is the island's favourite meeting point, with a barbecue and steelband music set with a stunning view as a backdrop.

The Blockhouse consists of barracks, magazines, cisterns, stables and cannon platforms set on the 400 feet high **Cape Shirley,** a magnificient lookout point.

Over one mile long **Dickenson Bay**, on the northwest coast is the most popular beach for tourists. The large number of hotels, restaurants and beach activities including sporting facilities are a major attraction.

PLACES TO VISIT WITH CHILDREN
St John`s - Capital
Museum - Old Court House Long Street, Open 6 days
Map Shop - St Mary's Street
Botanical Gardens - St John's
Betty's Hope Sugar Plantation - Main Road, Long Bay
Devil's Bridge - Indian Town Point, at the end of the road to Long Bay
Gayle's Ice Cream - Camacho's Avenue, Local - delicious flavours
Kentucky Fried Chicken - High Street and Fort Road
Brother B's - *West Indian Food,* Bank Alley
French Quarter - *Cajun/Caribbean*, Runaway Bay
Interpretation Centre - Dow's Hill,
Shirley Heights Complex - English Harbour
Shirley Heights Lookout - View of Nelson's Dockyard
Karibbean Kids - Redcliffe Quay
Toy Shop - Redcliffe Quay
Benetton - Heritage Quay
Naf-Naf - Heritage Quay
Body Shop - Heritage Quay

BARBUDA TOUR
Only fifteen minutes from Antigua by LIAT airline, the sister island Barbuda (pop. 1200) is an experience that should not be missed. For although, there are two exclusive resorts on Barbuda, the long established **Coco Point** and the relatively new **K Club** - which are regularly visited by those who have discovered this little paradise - too few Antiguan tourists make the effort.

The immediate impact upon the visitor to Barbuda is the flatness of the island. The second and most lasting impression is the incredible beauty and emptiness of the pink coral sand beaches and the colours of the surrounding sea.

Things to see are the **Frigate Bird**

Sanctuary, Codrington Village, Martello Tower and Fort, the Highlands, the caves and the many beaches which provide great snorkelling. For the best view of the island it is advisable to take a guided tour. People are very friendly and Barbuda gets very hot - so use care.

Day Tours

George Burton, Day Tours, Codrington Village, Barbuda, Tel: 460 0103/0221.

LIAT operate scheduled daily flights to Barbuda and special day trips can be organised by **LIAT's Travel Desk** in Antigua, Tel: 462 3142.

EVENTS

SAILING WEEK

Antigua Sailing Week is celebrated annually at the end of April. Over 300 of the world's finest sailing crafts converge for a week of serious racing and partying. By 1967 the original organisers and the Antigua Hotels Association had joined forces and extended the event to three full days of racing. Today yachts from all over the world sail to Antigua to race.

There are five races and many of these are not easily seen from land but there are strategic points from which it is possible to watch the spinnakers being released. Cruiser racing classes use spinnakers. This is a spectacular and breathtaking sight as the sea is awash with colour.

Apart from the competitive nature of racing there is also the serious business of partying. Each race ends with a beach celebration which continues into the night. Two days are set aside for organised fun and frolics - Lay Day and Dockyard Day - featuring beer drinking, wet T-shirt competitions, climbing the greasy pole, the tug-of-war and any other off-beat activity.

The non-mariners race is the highlight of Dockyard Day. The rules are simple; Contestants must construct a craft for less than EC$100. The competition rules stipulate that the craft must never have been in the water prior to the race.

Antigua Sailing Week is for sailing enthusiasts and party lovers and an excuse to have fun and watch or participate in one of the most renowned yachting events in the world.

For more information write or call: **The Secretary, Antigua Sailing Week, PO Box 406, St John's, Antigua.** Tel: 462-0036/6164. Fax: 462-2627

CARNIVAL

Antigua's carnival has been often described as the Caribbean's most colourful and exciting summer festival.

Carnival is about people having fun, an explosion of artistic and cultural talents, music, steelbands and calypso. Carnival is street parades and colourful costumes, bands and troupes.

Music, dance and camaraderie are the hallmark of Antigua's carnival. Held during the last week of July and culminating on the first Monday and Tuesday of August annually, carnival enjoys the participation of locals and visitors alike.

The planning starts early. "Mas Camps" design and build the gorgeous costumes months prior to carnival. Calypso singers plan, write and record their songs. Steelband members prepare their steelpans and arrangers plan the music for the steeldrums. Contestants for the Teenage Pageant, Carnival Queen's contest and Junior Calypso shows are selected and trained. By early June construction begins on the huge stage in carnival city.

In the weeks leading up to carnival the calypso tents open their doors at weekends and calypso lovers flock to sample the musical menu on offer.

Just prior to the official opening of carnival city, a festival village is set up with booths, blaring music and offering all manner of drinks and food for sale. The stage is now set -and carnival begins.

For the next 10 days the partying is almost non-stop. In carnival city the carnival committee arranges and produces a number of shows and activities

Outside carnival city there are street parades of costumed groups and endless nightly parties.

J'Overt, one of the highlights of people involvement in carnival starts at 4:00 am on the first Monday in August. To the music of steelbands, brassbands and hi-fi's people dance - jumpin' and jammin - on the streets of St John's. J'Overt is here.

The curtain on carnival comes down the following evening with the last lap - the final street jump-up which usually runs from 6.00 pm to midnight. And then it's back to normal.

For further information and details about taking part in carnival - contact: **The**

Carnival Office, Corn Alley, St John's, Antigua. Telephone 462-0194 or 462-4707

FINANCIAL INFORMATION

LOCAL TAX

For your convenience, a 10% service charge is automatically added to all accounts in lieu of gratuities; a 7% government tax is also added.

BANKS

Branches:
Antigua & Barbuda Development Bank, 27 St Mary's Street, Box 1279, St John's, Tel: 462-0838/9. Fax: 462-0839
Antigua Barbuda Investment Bank Ltd, High Street, Box 1679, St John's. Tel: 462-0067/1653. Fax: 462-0804
Antigua Commercial Bank, St Mary's & Thames Streets, Box 95, St John's. Tel: 462-1217/9/2085/1860/4. Fax: 462-1220
Barbuda Branch. Tel: 460-0066
VC Bird Intl Airport, Branch.Tel: 462-3052
Antigua Overseas Bank Ltd, High Street, Box 1679, St John's, Tel: 462-0067/1653
Bank of Antigua Ltd, Corner High & Thames Streets, Box 135, St John's, Tel: 462-4282 Fax: 462-4718.
Nelson's Dockyard Branch, Tel: 460-1367
Bank of Nova Scotia, Box 342, High Street, St John's,

Tel: 462-1104/06/08, Fax: 462-1578
Barclays Bank Plc, Box 225, High Street, St John's, Tel: 462-0334, Fax: 462 4910
St Mary's St Branch, Box 740, St John's Telephone: Tel: 462-0432, Fax: 462-1630
Canadian Imperial Bank of Commerce, High Street & Corn Alley, Box 28, St John's, Tel: 462-0836/7/0998
Caribbean Banking Corporation Ltd, High Street, Box 1324, St John's, Tel 462-4217, Fax: 462-5047
East Caribbean Central Bank, High Street, Tel: 462-2489/90
Guardian International Bank Ltd, Long Street, Box 315, St John's, Tel: 462-4283 Fax: 462-0040
International Bank & Trust Corp Ltd, Newgate Street, St John's, Tel: 462-3647
Royal Bank of Canada Ltd, High Street, Box 252, St John's, Tel: 462-0325/6. Fax: 462-1304
Swiss American Bank Ltd, High St., Box 1302, St John's. Fax: 462-0274.Tel: 462-4460/1. Business Development & Private

The Martello Tower and Fort, Barbuda

Banking, High St. St John's, Tel: 462-4477.
Heritage Quay (opens 9-4) Tel: 462-1637
Nelson's Dockyard : Tel: 460-1185/6/7.
Friar's Hill Road: Tel: 462-1755/6. Fax: 462-1831
Jolly Harbour: Tel: 462-7697/9. Fax: 462-7701.

EMERGENCY SERVICES

Emergencies - Tel: 999/911
Police - Tel: 462 0125
Fire - Tel: 462 0044
Hospital - Tel: 462 0251
Air/Sea Rescue - Tel: 462 3062
Ambulance - Tel: 462 0251
Electricity Faults - Tel: 311
Office of Disaster Preparedness - Tel: 462 4402

USEFUL TELEPHONE NUMBERS

Overseas Operator - Dial 0
Directory Assistance - Dial 411
VC Bird International Airport - Tel: 462 0528
Government offices (all depts) - Tel: 462 0003
Customs (collections) - Tel: 462 0026
Dockyard Office - Tel: 460 1479
Chamber of Commerce - Tel: 462 0743
Department of Tourism - Tel: 462 0029
Antigua Hotels & Tourism Association - Tel: 462 0374/3762
Cable & Wireless - Tel: 462 0078
United States Consulate - Tel 462 3505
British High Commission - Tel: 462 0008
AIRLINES - Reservations/Enquiries:
Air Canada - Tel: 462 1147,
Air St Kitts-Nevis - Tel: 465 8571
American Airlines - Tel: 462 0950,
British Airways - Tel: 462 0876,
BWIA - Tel: 462 0262/63/64,
Carib Aviation - Tel: 462 3147
Continental Airlines - Tel: 462 0323/24,
LIAT - Tel: 462 3142.
Lufthansa - Tel: 462 0983/87
Montserrat Airways - Tel: 491 6494/5342

HOTELS, GUEST HOUSES & APARTMENTS

Admirals Inn, Nelson's Dockyard, English Harbour, Box 713, St John's. Tel: 460-1027/1153. Fax: 460-1534

Antigua Beachcomber Hotel, Winthrops Bay, Coolidge, Box 10, St John's. Tel: 462-3100/4012 Fax: 462-2110

Antigua Sugar Mill Hotel, Coolidge, Box 319, St John's. Tel: 462-3044/0857. Fax: 462-1500/4790

Antigua Village Condominium Beach Resort, Dickenson Bay, Box 649, St John's, Antigua, Tel: 462-2930/4299. Fax: 462-0375

At-The-Hill Resort, Marble Hill, Box 30, St John's, Tel: 461 3312. Fax: 462 0527

Banana Cove Resort, Long Bay, Box 231, St John's. Tel: 463-2003/3302/3. Fax: 463-2425

Barrymore Beach Club, Runaway Bay, Box 1774, St John's. Tel: 462-4101 Fax: 462-4140

Barrymore Hotel, Fort Road, Box 1574, St John's. Tel: 462-1055, Fax: 462-4062

Blue Heron Hotel, Johnson's Point Beach, Box 1715, St John's. Tel: 462-8564/5/6/7 Fax: 462-8005

Blue Waters Beach Hotel, Soldiers Bay, Box 256, St John's. Tel: 462-0290/2, Fax: 462-0293

Bougainvillea Hotel, All Saints Road, Box 1236, St John's. Tel: 462-3040/1. Fax: 462-0225

Callaloo Beach Hotel, Old Road, Box 676, St John's. Tel: 462 8498/4, Fax: 462 8494

Camacho's John Central Hotel & Motoring Lodge, All Saint's Road, Box 273, St John's. Tel: 462 0489

Halfmoon Bay Hotel

Catamaran Hotel & Marina, Falmouth Harbour, Box 958. Tel: 460-1036/1503/1506, Fax: 460-1506

Club Antigua, Jolly Beach, Box 744, St John's. Tel: 462 0061, Fax 462 4900

Coco Point Lodge, Barbuda, Box 90, Hodges Bay. Tel: 462 3816

Copper & Lumber Store Hotel, Nelson's Dockyard, Box 184, English Harbour. Tel: 460-1058/1158/1159 Fax: 460-1529

Coral Sands, Runaway Bay, Box 34, Runaway Bay. Tel: 461-0925, Fax: 462-1187

Cornwall's Hotel, Camacho's Avenue, St John's. Tel: 462 1662

Cortsland Hotel, Upper Gambles, Box 403, St John's. Tel: 462-1395

Curtain Bluff Hotel, Old Road, Box 288, St John's. Tel: 462-8400/1/2, Fax: 462-8409

Deck Resort, English Harbour, Tel :460 1719

Diamond Rock Resort, Redcliffe Quay, Tel 462 1401

Dian Bay Resort, Long Bay, Tel: 463 2425

Dickenson Bay Cottages. Tel: 462 4940

Falmouth Beach Apartments, Falmouth Harbour, Box 713, St John's. Tel: 460-1027/1094 Fax: 460-1534

Galleon Beach, Freeman's Bay, English Harbour, Box 1003, St John's. Tel: 460-1024, Fax: 460-1450

Galley Bay Hotel, Five Islands, Box 305, St John's. Tel: 462-0302, Fax:462-4551

Halcyon Cove Beach Resort, Dickenson Bay, Box 251, St John's. Tel: 462-0256/7, Fax: 462-0271

Half Moon Bay Hotel, Box 144, St John's, Tel 460 4300, Fax 460 4306

Harbour View Apartments, Falmouth Harbour, Box 20, All Saints. Tel: 460-1762, Fax: 809-460-1871

Hawksbill Beach Resort, Five Islands, Box 108, St John's. Tel: 462-0301, Fax: -462-1515

Heritage Hotel, Heritage Quay, Box 1532, St John's. Tel: 462-1247, Fax: 462-1179

Hodges Bay Club Resort, Hodges Bay, Box 1237, St John's. Tel: 462-2300 Fax: 462-1962

Inn At English Harbour, English Harbour, Box 187, St John's. Tel: 460-1014, Fax: 460-1603

Island Inn, Anchorage Road, Box 1218, St John's, Tel: 462 4065, Fax: 462 4066

Joe Mike's Hotel Plaza, Box 136, St John's. Tel: 462-1142/3244 Fax: 462-6056

Joseph's Jolly Castle Hotel, Jolly Harbour. Tel: 462-7425

Jolly Harbour Beach Resort, Jolly Harbour, Box 1793, St John's. Tel: 462-6166, Fax: 462-6167

Jumby Bay Club, Long Island, Box 243. Tel: 462-6000 Fax: 462-6020

K Club, Barbuda, Tel: 460 0300, Fax 460 0305

Lapps Airport Road Hotel, Airport Road, Tel: 462 1191, Fax 462 0928

Long Bay Hotel, Long Bay, Box 442, St John's. Tel: 463-2005, Fax: 463-2439

Lord Nelson Beach Hotel, Dutchman's Bay, Box 155, St John's. Tel: 462-3094, Fax: 462-0751

Marina Bay Resort, Corbinsons Point, Dickenson Bay, Box 1407, St John's. Tel: 462-3254/5/8, Fax: 462-2151

Murphy's Place, All Saints Road. Tel: 461-1183

Miami Hotel & Supermarket, Market Street, Box 300, St John's. Tel:462 0975

Mill Reef Club, Mill Reef. Tel: 462 2081/ 2/4290/9

Paradise Guest House, Cnr Camacho's Ave & Edward Street, St John's. Tel: 462 1904

Pigotsville Hotel, Box 521, St John's, Tel 462 0592

Pillar Rock Hotel & Condominiums, Deep Bay, Box 1266, St John's, Tel:462 2326/2623. Fax 462 2327

Pineapple Beach Club, Long Bay, Box 54, St John's. Tel: 463-2006/2451, Fax: 463-2452

Popeshead Guest House, Popeshead Street, Box 1465. Tel: 462 3600

Ramada Renaissance Royal Antiguan Resort, Deep Bay, Box 1322, St John's, Tel 462 3733/4/5, Fax: 462 3732

Roslyn's Guest House, Fort Road, Box 161, St John's, Tel: 462 0762

Runaway Beach Club, Runaway Bay, Box 874, St John's. Tel: 462-2650/1/2, Fax: 462-4172

Sand Haven Hotel, Box 405, Sand Haven, St John's, Tel: 462 4491/3286, Fax: 462 3334

St. James's Club, Mamora Bay, Box 63, St John's. Tel: 460-5000, Fax: 460-3015

Sandals Antigua, Dickenson Bay, Box 147, Tel: 462-0267. Fax: 462-4135

Siboney Beach Club, Dickenson Bay, Box 222, St John's, Tel: 462-2155/0806, Fax: 462-3356

Silver Dollar Guest House, All Saints Road. Tel: 462 3554

St John's Motel, Fort Road, Tel: 462 1448

St Mary's Court Hotel, St Mary's Street, Box 1327, St John's, Tel: 462 4770

Stephendale Hotel, Fort Road, St John's, Tel: 462 1366

Sunjet View Hotel, Codrington, Barbuda, Tel: 460 0005

Sunset Cove Resort, Runaway Bay, Box 1262, St John's. Tel: 462-3762, Fax: 462-2684

Sunset View Resort, Belle Village, Barbuda, Tel: 460 0078

Thomas House, Barbuda. Tel: 460 0004

Time-A-Way, Runaway Bay, Box 189, St Johns. Tel: 462-0775/1212/ 3367

Trade Winds Cove, Box 165, St John's. Tel: 461-0111, Fax: 462-3772

Trade Winds Hotel & Apartments, Dickenson Bay,Box 1390, St John's. Tel: 462-1223, Fax: 462-5007

Trafalgar Beach Villas, Pillar Rock Beach, Deep Bay, Box 1585, St John's. Tel: 462-2531/2548, Fax: 462-2531

Yepton Beach Resort, Hog John Bay, Box 1427, St Johns. Tel: 462-2520, Fax: 462-3240

EATING OUT
LOCAL DELICACIES

Souse. This is boiled pork marinated in water and lime-juice with onions, peppers, garlic and cucumber. It is served with lettuce and tomatoes and eaten with hot bread rolls.

Salt Fish. This is the traditional Antiguan Sunday morning breakfast dish. It is dried cod which has been soaked, boiled and boned, in a rich onion and tomato sauce. As a breakfast dish it is usually accompanied by Doucouna, a small pudding made from grated sweet potato and coconut mixed with flour and spices and boiled in a banana leaf.

Pepper Pot. This is a rich delicious stew containing salt beef, pork, pumpkin, paw-paw, spinach, peas, aubergines and okras, with onion, garlic and spices. It can be served with dumplings or with a cornmeal pudding known as Fungee.

Conch Stew. Another excellent stew prepared with the large shellfish called conch. The meat has to be tenderised before being cooked with onions, tomatoes and spices.

These and other local dishes are served by specialised restaurants.

RESTAURANTS & BARS

Most hotels have restaurants and it is advisable to make a reservation

Abracadabra, *Italian*, Nelson's Dockyard, English Harbour, Tel: 460-1732

Admiral's Inn, *International/West Indian*, Nelson's Dockyard, Tel: 460-1027/1153, Fax: 460-1534

Alberto's, *Italian*,Willoughby Bay, Tel: 460-3007

Al Porto Ristorante & Bar, Jolly Harbour, Tel: 462-7695

Andes Restaurant & Bar, *Seafood/ Caribbean*, Royal Antiguan Resort, Tel: 462-3733

Almond Tree Restaurant, Banana Cove, Long Bay, Box 231, St John's, Tel: 463 2003

Antigua Yacht Club, English Harbour, Tel: 460 1444

Barry Cudas Restaurant, Fun Food, Jaws Restaurant , Five Islands, Tel: 462-2428

Beachcomber Hotel, Bar & Restaurant, Coolidge, Tel: 462 3100

Big Bamboo, Newgate Street, St John's, Tel:462.0605

Big Bite, *Indian/West Indian*, Long Street, Tel: 462-2949

Billgins Bar & Restaurant, Camachos Avenue, Tel: 462 3556

Boston's Restaurant, Michael's Avenue, St John's, Tel: 462 4510

Brother B's, *West Indian/Seafood*, Long Street, Tel: 462 0616

Brother D`s Restaurant, Donald Watkins, Kentish Road, Tel: 462 3645

Brown Sugar Restaurant, *West Indian/International*, Antigua Sugar Mill Hotel, Tel: 462-0857/3044

Buccaneer Cove, *Seafood/West Indian*, Dickenson Bay, Tel: 462-2173/0959

Burger Hut Snack Bar, Union Road, Tel: 462 2712

Bush Garden Bar & Restaurant, Golden Grove, Box 960, St John's, Tel: 461 2881

C Front Restaurant & Bar, Crabbs Slipway, Box 271, St John's, Tel: 463 2604

Cacubi Room, *Nouvelle Caribbean Cuisine*, Blue Waters Beach Hotel, Soldiers Bay, Tel: 462-0290/0292

Cafe Club, *French,* Corner Church Street & Corn Alley, Tel: 462 4766

Calypso Restaurant, *West Indian/Seafood*, Redcliffe Street, Tel: 462-1965

Chez Pascal French Restaurant & Cocktail Lounge, Cross & Tanner Streets, Tel: 462 3232

China Garden Restaurant, Market Street, Tel: 462-2874

China Restaurant, St Mary's Street, Tel: 461 6463

Clouds Restaurant, Dickenson Bay, Tel: 462-0256/7

Commissioner Grill, *International/West Indian*, Commissioner Alley, Tel: 462-1856

Cockleshell Inn, Lower Fort Road, Tel: 462-0471

Coconut Grove, Siboney Beach Club, Dickenson Bay, Tel: 462-1538/2162

Colombo's Italian Restaurant, Galleon Beach Club, English Harbour, Tel: 460-1452

Creole Cottage, South Street, Tel: 462-6174

Curry House, Box 1247, Redcliffe Quay, Tel: 462 1895

Curtain Bluff Hotel, *International*, Old Road, Tel: 462 8400

Crazy Cactus Cantina, *Mexican*, All Saints Road, St John's, Tel: 461-1183

D D's Dinner & Bar, DeSouza Road, Tel: 462-3260

Daddy`s Boy, *Fast Food*, Nevis Street, St John's

Darcy`s Bar & Restaurant, *West Indian*, St Mary's Street, Tel: 462-1323

Delightful Restaurant, St Mary's Street, Tel: 462-5780

The Deck, *West Indian*, English Harbour, Tel: 460-1719

The Docksider, *Seafood/West Indian*, St James's Club. Tel: 460-5000

Dogwatch Tavern, *English Pub*, Jolly Harbour Beach Resort, Tel: 462 6550

Dolphin Restaurant & Bar, All Saints Road, Tel: 462-1183

Dubarry's Restaurant, Fort Road, Tel: 462-4063/1055

Dubliner Bar & Restaurant, *Caribbean/International*, Lower Redcliffe Street, Tel: 462 6339

Famous Mauros Bar & Restaurant Pizzeria, English Harbour, Tel: 460 1318

Fish House Restaurant, Upper Newgate Street, Tel: 462-6028

Fisherman`s Wharf, *Seafood/Westindian*, Heritage Quay, Tel: 462 2248

Franks Strand Cafe, *International*, Barrymore Beach Resort, Runaway Bay, Tel: 462-4139

French Quarter Restaurant & Night Club, *Cajun/American*, Runaway Bay Tel: 462-0624/2783

G & T Pizza, *Italian,* English Harbour, Tel: 460-3278

Galley Restaurant, Nelson's Dockyard, English Harbour. Tel: 460 1533

The Garden, *International*, Blue Waters Beach Resort, Tel: 462 0290/0292

Germain's Bar & Restaurant, *West Indian/American*, Dollar Building, Nevis St. Tel: 462-2967

Golden Boat, *Oriental*, English Harbour, Tel: 460-3337

Goldstar Bar & Restaurant, All Saints Road, Tel: 462-0439

Grace Before Meals, *Fast Food*, English Harbour, Tel: 460-1298

Halcyon Cove Beach Resort, Dickenson Bay, Tel: 462-0256/7

Harbour Cafe, *French/Spanish/Brazilian*, Jolly Harbour, Tel: 462 6026

Harbour View Bar & Restaurant, Market Street, Tel: 462-2775

Harmony Hall, *Caribbean/Seafood*, Freetown, Tel: 460-4120

Hawksbill Beach Resort, *European/West Indian*, Tel: 462 0301

Hemmingway's Caribbean Cafe, *International/Caribbean*, St Mary's Street, St John's, Tel: 462-2763

Home Restaurant, *Caribbean*, Luther George Place, Gambles Terrace, Tel: 461-7651

Hong Kong Restaurant, Newgate Street, St John`s, Tel: 462 3444

Inn At English Harbour, *International/West Indian*, Terrace & Beach Restaurant, English Harbour, Tel: 460-1014,

Island Cafe, *Caribbean*, Fort Road, St John`s Tel 462 2977

Jacinta's Restaurant & Snack Bar, *West Indian*, Lower Market Street, St John's.

Jaws Restaurant & Entertainment Lounge, *International*, Five Islands, Tel: 462-2428

Kentucky Fried Chicken, Cnr High & Thames Streets, Tel: 462 1951/2. Fort Road, St John's, Tel: 462-1973/4

Kim Do Restaurant, 28 Cross Street, Tel: 462-5776

Kim Sha Bar & Restaurant, *Chinese*, Church Street, St John's, Tel: 462-4505

Ko-zee Cocktail Lounge & English Pub, Fort James Road, Tel: 461-5873

Kwik Stop Restaurant, *West Indian/Creole*, English Harbour. Tel: 460 1299

La Dolce Vita Restaurant & Bar, *Italian*, Redcliffe Quay, St John`s, Tel: 462-2016

Lagoon Cafe & Restaurant, *West Indian*, Codrington Village, Barbuda, Tel: 460-0439

L'Auberge de Paris, Dickenson Bay, Tel: 462-1223

Le Bistro, *French/ Italian*, Box 390, Hodges Bay. Tel: 462-3881, 461-2996

Le Cap Horn, *French/Argentinian*, English Harbour, Tel: 460-1194

Lemon Tree, *International*, Long Street, Tel: 462-1969/0777

Limeys Bar & Restaurant, *West Indian*, Nelsons Dockyard, Tel: 460-1144

Little Conton Restaurant, Bishopgate Street, Tel: 462-3298

Little Kristal Restaurant, Bishopgate, Tel: 462-0538

Lobster Pot, *Seafood specialities*, Runaway Bay, Box 1370, St John's, Tel: 462-2855/6/464-0928

Lagoon Cafe, *West Indian*, Royal Antiguan Hotel, Tel: 462-3733

La Perruche, *French/West Indian*, Tel: 460-3040

Miller's By The Sea, *Seafood/West Indian*, Dickenson Bay, Tel: 462-2393

Mainbrace Pub, English Harbour, Tel: 460 1058

Malone`s Creole Restaurant, English Harbour, Tel: 460 1570

Munchies Cafe & Meat Shop, Old Parham Road, Tel: 462-2186

Maracuja, *International/Health Food*, Falmouth Harbour, Tel: 460-2702

The Nook, St Mary's Street, Tel: 462 1158

Ocean Blend Bar & Restaurant, Deep Water Harbour, Tel: 462-1716

Orient Restaurant, Popeshead Street, Tel: 462-3757

The Orchid, *Oriental*, Royal Antiguan, Tel: 462-3732

Pam's Snackette, Brownes Ave, Tel: 462-4459

Pari's Pizza, *Italian/International*, St John's, Tel: 462-1501

Patio Caribe, *Continental/Caribbean*, Deep Bay. Tel: 462-2520

Pavillion Restaurant At Pillar Rock, *Italian/Continental*, Deep Bay, Tel: 462-2325

Pelican Club Restaurant, *Continental/West Indian*, Hodges Bay, Tel: 462-2300

Piccolo Mondo, *Italian*, St James's Club, Tel: 460-5000

Phil's Crocodile Restaurant & Bar, Long Bay, Tel: 463-2003

Pirate & Parrot Fisherman's Corner & "Fun" Restaurant, Heritage Quay, St John's, Tel: 462-3558/9/7

Pirates Den Box, 165 Upper Nevis St, St John's, Tel: 462-4508

Pitch Bar & Restaurant, c/o Jonas Foster, Tel: 461-1417

Pizzas On The Quay, *Italian*, Redcliffe Quay, Tel: 462-2621

Quencher, *West Indian/international/Fast Food*, Redcliffe Quay, St John's. Tel: 462-1941

Raskalls on Church, *West Indian/International*, Church Street, St John`s, Tel: 462 0016

Redcliffe Tavern, *International*, Redcliffe Quay, St John's, Tel: 461-4557

Rendezvous Restaurant, Horsford Hill, English Harbour, Tel: 460-2117

Royal Palm Restaurant & Bar, Tanner & Cross St, Tel: 462-3232

Rainbow Garden, *Continental*, Tel: 460-5000

Rookery, *International/French/West Indian*, Blue Heron Hotel. Tel: 462-8564

Sand Haven Restaurant & Lounge, *Continental*, Sand Haven, Tel: 462-4438

Shirley Heights Lookout, *West Indian/Seafood*, overlooking Nelson's Dockyard. Tel: 460-1785

Shooters at Tradewinds, Dickenson

Bay, Tel: 462 1501
Snack Shak, Old Parham Road, Tel: 462-3846
Speedy Joe's, *Fast Food*, Nevis Street,Tel: 462-1142/3244
Spice Bar Restaurant & Arcade, Prince Klass Street, Tel: 462-4732
Spinnakers Beach Bar & Restaurant, Dickenson Bay, Tel: 462-4158
St James's Club, Mamora Bay, Tel: 460-5000
Stephanies, c/o Pasty, Hodge Street, Johnsons Blvd. Tel: 462-3245
Stoplight Restaurant & Bar, Kentish Road, Tel: 462-0633
Surf & Turf Restaurant, Five Islands, Tel: 462-0301
Southern Fry, *Creole*. Tel: 462-2616
Steely Bar & Gourmet Corner, *International*, Jolly Harbour, Tel: 462-1781
Toby's, *West Indian*, Main Road, Long Bay. Tel: 463-3251
To Go, *Take-out Fast Food*, Redcliffe Quay.
Tokyo Seafood House, *Japanese/Chinese*, Deep Water Harbour, Tel: 464-6400
Talk Of The Town Restaurant, Redcliffe Street, Tel: 462-0535
Tutti Frutti, High Street, Tel: 462-0295
Udder Delight, *Ice Cream Parlour*, Heritage Quay. Tel: 462-2248
Vietnamese Restaurant, Hodges Bay, Tel: 462-3293
Vienna Beach Restaurant & Bar, *International*, Johnson's Point, Tel: 462-1442
Wah Fung, Bar & Restaurant, English Harbour, Tel: 463-3337

Willy's Roast, Long Street, Tel: 462-4611
Warri Pier, *Seafood/Grill/International*, Halcyon Cove Hotel; Dickenson Bay, Tel: 462-0256
Wardroom, *International*, Nelson`s Dockyard, Tel: 460 1058
West Indian Coffee & Tea Shop, Jolly Harbour, Tel: 462 6216

NIGHT LIFE
NIGHTCLUBS & CASINOS
Charisma Nite Club, Fort Road, St. John's. Tel: 462-1449
Club Antigua, Jolly Beach. Tel: 462 0061
Jackpot Casino Slots, Asot's Arcade, 18 High Street, St. John's. Tel: 462-2359
Joe Mikes Casino-Arcade, Corn Alley. Tel: 462-6056

King's Casino, Heritage Quay, St. John's. Tel: 462-1727
Shirley Heights Lookout, Shirley Heights. Tel: 460-1785
The Warehouse, Redcliffe Quay, St. John's. Tel: 462-2317
Lime Antigua, Redcliffe Quay Tel: 461 4557

SHOPPING
Duty Free Shops
Scent Shop, High Street, Box 272, St John's. Tel: 462-0303.
V. C. Bird International Airport, Tel: 462-3162
Speciality Shoppe - Crystal, China Jewellery & Silverware, St Mary's Street, Box 1693, St John's. Tel: 462-1198.

There are four main shopping areas: HERITAGE QUAY, REDCLIFFE QUAY, JOLLY HARBOUR SHOPPING CENTRE and central St. JOHN'S.

HERITAGE QUAY, St. Mary's Street.
Beach Stuff Tel: 462 3610
Benetton Tel: 462 3273
Best Price Display Tel: 462 1782
The Body Shop Tel: 462 2810
Caribbean Gems Tel: 462 3670
Caribbean Trading Best
The Cigar Shop Tel: 462 2677
Colombian Emeralds Tel: 462 3462/3351
Decibels
Craft Emporium Tel: 462 3618
European Imports Tel: 462 3614
Glenette's Cosmetic Center Tel: 462 1700
Gucci Tel: 462 2890
Heritage Sports Tel: 462 2809
Island Arts Tel: 462 2787

J.C.M. Jewellers Ltd. Tel: 462 4397/8
Joanette Boutique Tel: 462 3613
La Boutique Elegance, Tel:
La Parfumerie Tel: 462 2601/3
The "Land" Shop Tel: 462 0746
Laureen's Boutique Tel: 462 5552
The Linen Shop Tel: 462 3611
Little Switzerland Tel: 462 3108
Naf-Naf International Tel: 462 2608/9
Norma's Duty-Free Shop Tel: 462 0172
Picks of Paridise
Quin Farara Tel: 462 1737
Radio Shack, Tel: 462 2685
See Jays and Sons Le Chateau
Saddlers
Shipwreck Shop Tel: 462 3621
Shock Tel: 462 4964
Sunseakers Tel: 462 3618
Tropic Wear
Wadadli Smoke Booze Tel: 462 2606
West Indies Ice Co Tel: 462 2343
Windjammer Clothing Co. Tel: 462 0746
World of Leather, Tel: 462 3168

**JOLLY HARBOUR MARINA AND
SHOPPING CENTRE**
Shops normally open 9.00 to 5.00 daily
unless otherwise stated.
Beach Stuff Tel: 462 7710
El Caribe Tel: 462 6087
E&F Gifts & Souvenirs Tel: 462 6905
ETI Tel: 462 3087
Electrotek Ltd
The Flower Basket Tel: 462 7708
Franco
In Vogue Tel: 462 7693
Jacaranda Tel: 462 7689
La Parfumerie Tel: 462 6217
Merry Gift Shop Tel: 4627712
Quin Farara Tel: 462 6245
Seahorse Studios

Day Charters
Kokomo Cat - day cruise on a catamaran.
Music, food and drinks. Tel: 462 7245.
La Marine - water taxi service and small
boat charters. Tel: 462 7686.

Food & Beverage
Quin Farara - wines and spirits merchant
Tel: 462 6245.
Marine Services
A1 Marine Maintenance - diesel engine
sales, service and repair - other
engineering services.
Alwgrip Antigua - specialists in Spray
painting and osmosis .
Budget Marine - chandlery, Tel: 462 7727.
Burton's Laundry - full services and do it
yourself. (in the Boatyard).
Dockside Services - Travel agents, Car
hire agency & business services. Tel: 462
7595.
Harbour Woodworks - wood fabrication
and general repairs to equipment. Tel: 462
7715.
Harris Boat Works - boat painting repair,
maintenance and refurbishing.
Marionics Ltd. - Marine electronics -
sales, services and repair. Tel: 462 6041.
Jolly Harbour Marina - full service marina
with 70-ton travel llift, 150-slip boatyard.
Texaco Starport fuel dock. Tel: 462 6041/2.
North Coast Marine - power boat sales,
service & repair. Agents for Mercury/
Mercruiser/marine and Quicksilver.
Tel:462 4886/6083.
Restaurants
Al Porto Ristorante & Bar - pizzas, pasta
and sea food. Tel: 462 7695
Cafe Journal & Frank's Bakery &
Cafeteria, breakfast, lunch, dinner,
Caribbean & International Tel: 462 7716.
Harbour Cafe - Creole , local, Salads,
sandwiches Tel: 462 6026.
Steely Bar and Gourmet Corner - inside
Sports Centre. Specials & international.
Entertainment after dark with 150" live

screen. Tel: 462 6260, VHF 68.
West Indian Coffee and Tea Shop coffee,
sandwiches, pastries, cakes. Tel: 462
6216.
The Dogwatch Tavern - Pub-style bar &
restaurant. Tel: 462 6550.

Services
Postal Box Rentals - Tel: 462 3085.
Swiss American Bank - a full service
bank. Tel: 462 7697.
The Cutting Edge - international unisex
hair stylists. Skin and manicure services.
Tel: 462 7709.
The Photo Shop - photographic and video
equipment including film, tape, batteries
and 24- hour processing. Tel: 462 7726.
Sports
Antigua Bait & Tackle Shop - fishing
equipment and live bait.   Tel: 462
6320.
BBR Sportive - 4 tennis courts,
international squash court, 25 metre
swimming pool. Tel: 462 6260, VHF 68.
Jolly Dive - full diving services including
instructions. Diving equipment for sale.
Tel: 462 8305.
Villa Sales & Rentals
Jolly Harbour Villa Rentals - short term
rentals of fully furnished waterfront villas.
Tel: 462 6166. Fax: 462 6167.
Jolly Harbour Villa Sales & Management
- Waterfront villas for sale. Tel: 462 7595.
or Fax: 462 7703.
Shopping Centre Information - Geoffrey
Pidduck, P.O. Box 1559, Jolly Harbour.
Tel 462 7595 Fax: 462-7703.

REDCLIFFE QUAY
Redcliffe Street, shops are open daily
from 9 to 5. unless stated otherwise.
Base Antigua Tel: 462 0920
Bona Tel: 462 2036

Calypso Tel: 462 1374
Dalila Tel: 462 3625
Decibels Tel: 462 0632
Gifts & Baskets
Gifts for Pleasure
The Goldsmitty Tel: 462 4601
Island Woman
Jacaranda
Karibbean Kids of Antigua,
Potpourri
Seahorse Studios
Things Caribbean
Toucan Crafts & Gifts
The Toy Shop
A Thousand Flowers
Tropical Edition
Video Town
Visions of Antigua

ST JOHN'S AND ELSEWHERE

Abdo Mansoor & Sons,
Anabelle's Boutique,
John & Francis Anjo
B's Formal & Rental
Gigi Plaza, Market Street.
Bailey's Countryside Flowers,
Beach Stuff, Temo Sports, English Harbour
Bernadette's Beauty Salon & Gift Center at Joe Mike's Hotel Plaza on Corn Alley.
Bessie's Variey Store, Cobb's Cross
Blue Waters Gift Shop, Blue Waters Hotel
Lionel Boulos, Long Street
Cadman's Creations
Cheryl Jeanery & Rambo Jam Can Record Shop, Market Square
Cockleshell Pottery, Lower Fort Road
CoCo Shop, St. Mary's Street and at V.C.Bird International Airport
Coconuts, located at Bob Camacho's Arcade, High Street
The Cohobblopot, Church Street.
Company's Coming, Church Street

SUPERMARKETS

Antigua Public Store, Market Street. Tel: 462-1659
Bailey's Supermarket, Falmouth Harbour. Tel: 460-1142
Benjamins'Supermarket, Sea View Farm. Tel: 463-1101
Brysons Supermarket, Long Street, St John's. Tel: 462-2136
Carib Marine Ltd, English Harbour, St John's. Tel: 460-1521
Christo's Supermarket, High Street, St John's. Tel: 462-1268
Cornwall's Wholesale Supermarket & Hotel, Camacho's Ave. Tel: 462-1662
De Freitas Supermarket, Camacho's Ave, St John's. Tel: 461-1629
Destin's Supermarket, North Street, St John's. Tel: 462-1166
Epicurean The, Old Parham Road, St John's. Tel: 462-2565
Food Brokerage Services Ltd, Newgate Street. Tel: 462-2187 and on South Street 462-4407
Food City, Deep Water Harbour, St John's. Tel: 462-4808
Gloria's Supermarket, Wenner Road. Tel: 462-4100
Grahams Supermarket & Wholesale, Old Parham Road, St John's. Tel: 462-4545/6196
Grant H C-Caribbean Wholesale Agency, Sheppard Street, St Michael Village, St John's, Tel: 462-3992,
Joseph Lane - 462-4957, Radio Range, Tel: 461-6361
Joseph's Supermarket, Jolly Harbour, Tel: 462-7425
Harbour Supermarket & Deli, Jolly Harbour. Tel: 462-7705
Henny's Superette, Barbuda. Tel: 460-0294
Highway Food Store, All Saints Road, St John's. Tel: 462-0903
Hutchinson's Supermarket, Old Parham Road. St John's. Tel: 462-2007

Jarvis Supermarket, Tindale Road, St John's. Tel: 462-2793/1164
Jeffrey's Supermarket, Golden Grove. Tel: 462-2873
L & S Supermarket, Yorks. Tel: 461-2981
La Superette, Wilikies Village. Tel: 463-3459
Little Giant Supermarket, All Saints Road. Tel: 462-2945
London House Supermarket, Long Street. Tel: 462-3595
London Store, All Saints Road. Tel: 462-0975
Meade's Supermarket, Bennett Street, St John's. Tel: 462-0470
Merchant's Silver Lining Supermarket, Ottos Main Road. Tel: 462-3721
NSW Supermarket, Newgate Street, St John's. Tel: 462-1498
Nearby Market, Ottos Main Road, St John's. Tel: 462-0689
Northshore Inn & Supermarket, Cedar Grove. Tel: 462-0098
O'Beez Food Store, Factory Road, St John's. Tel: 462-4660
Pond View Superette, Old Road Village. Tel: 462-8617
Richardson's Supermarket, Kentish Road. Tel: 462-0479
Rock Aan Sun Supermarket, Potters. Tel: 462-2373
Sammy Self Service, All Saints Road. Tel: 462-2195
Shoprite Supermarket, Fort Road, St John's. Tel: 462-3923
Shortcuts Superette, Cross Street. Tel: 462-2334
Silver Lining Supermarket, Ottos Main Road, St John's. Tel: 462-3721
Stanmar Supermarket, Market Square, St John's. Tel: 462-3421
Tasty Foods Ltd., Old Parham Road, St John's. Tel: 462-1931
U J's Surprise Supermarket, Golden Grove. Tel: 462-4791
U Supermarket, Cross & Nevis Streets, Tel: 462-2745

West Alister, De Souza Road, St John's.
Tel: 462-1256
Wyre Arnold, All Saints Road, St John's.
Tel: 461-0903
Zephy's Food Store, All Saints Road. Tel:
462-3539

PHOTOGRAPHY
Island Studios, *Commercial/Underwater,*
Redcliffe Street, Box 658, St John's. Tel:
462 1567/2066. Fax: 462 1567

BOOK & MAGAZINE SHOPS
Adventist Book Centre, Ottos New
Town, St John's. Tel: 462 4546
Books At Redcliffe Quay, 23 Redcliffe
Quay, St John's. Tel: 462 0589
Caribbean Educational Services Ltd, St
Mary's Street, Box 469, St John's. Tel:
462 3993. Fax: 462 3993
Christian Literature Centre, Lower
Church Street, Box 203, St John's. Tel:
462 2024. Fax: 462 2023
The Flower Basket, Gregory Building,
Nevis Street, Box 1047, St John's. Tel:
462 0411. Fax: 462 0411
Gerona Books & Variety Store,
Popeshead Street. Tel: 462 0878
Island Newsstand, Bob Camacho's
Arcade, Lower High Street, St John's. Tel:
462 2457. Fax: 462 2458
The Map Shop, St Mary's Street, Box
469, St John's. Tel: 462 3993. Fax: 462
3993
Methodist & Book Shop, St Mary's
Street, St John's. Tel: 462 3864
P C's Book Revue, St Mary's Street, St
John's. Tel: 462 1545
Schooltext & Supplies, High Street, Box
918, St John's. Tel: 462 2911

FURTHER INFORMATION
For more information on visiting Antigua
and Barbuda, contact the Department of

Tourism office closest to you:
*Antigua & Barbuda Department of
Tourism*, 610 Fifth Avenue, Suite 311,
New York, NY 10020 USA. Tel: 212-541-
4117
*Antigua & Barbuda Department of
Tourism*, 60 St. Clair Avenue East Suite
305, **Toronto**, Ontario, Canada M4T 1N5.
TEl: 416-961-3085
Antigua Department of Tourism, Thames
Street, P.O. Box 363, **St. John's**, Antigua.
Tel: 809-462-0480
Antigua & Barbuda Department of

Tourism & Trade, Antigua House, 15
Thayer Street, **London** W1M 5DL. Tel:
071-486-7073
Consulate of Antigua & Barbuda, 905 Star
House, 3 Salisbury Road, Tsimshatsui,
Kowloon, **Hong Kong**. Tel: 852-736-8033
Antigua & Barbuda Trade Mission, 304
International Drive NW, Suite 4M,
Washington, DC 20008 USA. Tel: 202-
362-5122
Antigua & Barbuda German Office,
Postfach 1331, Minnholzweg 2, 6242
Kronberg 1, Germany. Tel:06173/7091-11

ANTIGUA & BARBUDA A Little Bit of Paradise **QUICK GUIDE**

BIBLIOGRAPHY

Anonymous, Antigua and the Antiguans Vols. I & II, (Saunders and Otley, London, 1844)

Aspinall, Sir Algernon, A Wayfarer in the West Indies, (Methuen & Co, London, 1934)

Campbell, Kenneth (ed.), Antigua and Barbuda Supplement in Westindian Digest, (Hansib Publishing, London, November 1986)

de Fortis, Paul (ed.), The Kingdom of Redonda: 1865-1990, (The Aylesworth Press, England, 1991)

Dookhan, Issac A Post-Emancipation History of the West Indies, (Collins, England, 1985)

Dunn, Richard S., Sugar and Slaves: the Rise of the Planter Class in the English West Indies, 1624-1713, (The Norton Library, New York, 1973)

Dyde, Brian, Antigua and Barbuda: The Heart of the Caribbean, (Macmillan Caribbean, 1986)

Davis, Gregson & Davis, Margo, Antigua Black, (Scrimshaw Press, San Francisco, 1973)

Emmanuel, Patrick A., Elections & Party Systems in the Commonwealth Caribbean, 1944-1991, (Caribbean Development Research Services, Barbados,1992)

Eves, C. Washington, The West Indies, (Sampson Low, Marston & Company, 1897)

Graves, Charles, Fourteen Islands in the Sun, (Leslie Frewin, London, 1965)

Hall, Douglas, Five of the Leewards:1834-1870, (Gin & Company, Bucks, UK, 1971)

Harlow, Vincent T., Christopher Codrington 1668-1710 (Hurst & Company. London, 1990)

Jane, Charles W. E., Shirley Heights: The Defence of Nelson's Dockyard, (Reference Library of Nelson's Dockyard National Park Foundation, Antigua)

Laurence, K. O., Immigration into the West Indies in the 19th Century, (Gin & Company Ltd, England, 1971)

Lowenthal, David & Clarke, Colin G., Slave Breeding in Barbuda: The Past of a Negro Myth, (Annals of the New York Academy of Sciences, Volume 292, pp 510-535, 27 June 1977)

Lowenthal, David & Clarke, Colin G., "Common Lands, Common Aims: The Distinctive Barbudan Community", in Peasants Plantations & Rural Communities in the Caribbean, (Cross & Marks (eds), University of Surrey, 1979)

Lloyd, Paul C., Historic Architecture: design guidelines for a historic district; St John's Antigua, (1984)

Nicholson, D. V., et al, Antigua: Reefs, Rocks & Highroads of History, (Leeward Islands Science Associates, Antigua 1986)

Nicholson, D. V., Place Names in Antigua and Barbuda, (Antigua Archaeological & Historical Society, July 1984)

Pocock, Tom, Horatio Nelson, (Bodley Head, London, 1987)

Pocock, Tom, The Young Nelson in the Americas, (Collins, London, 1980)

Prince, Ralph (ed.), Antigua and Barbuda 1834-1984: From Bondage to Freedom; 150th Anniversary of Emancipation, (Ministry of Economic Development, Tourism & Energy, Antigua, 1984)

Richards, Novelle H., The Struggle & The Conquest, (Workers Voice Printery, Antigua, undated)

Richards, Novelle H., The Struggle & The Conquest Part II: The Locust Years, (Benjies Printery, Antigua, 1981)

Sanders, Ron (ed.), Antigua and Barbuda Official Independence Magazine, (Ministry of Foreign Affairs, Antigua 1981)

Sanders, Ronald, An End to Racism, A Beginning of Humanism: Lessons from Slavery and Servitude, (Caribbean Communications, Surrey, England, 1984)

Sanders, Ronald, Antigua and Barbuda 1966-1981: Transition Trial Triumph, (Archives Committee, Antigua, July 1984)

Schoultz, Lars, National Security and United States Policy toward Latin America, (Princeton University Press, New Jersey, 1987)

Smith, Keithlyn B. & Fernando C., To Shoot Hard Labour: The Life and Times of Samuel Smith, an Antiguan workingman 1877-1982, (Edan's Publishers, Canada, 1986)

Sturge, Joseph & Harvey, Thomas, The West Indies in 1837 (Hamilton, Adams & Company, England, 1838)

Waugh, Alec, The Sunlit Caribbean, (Evans Brothers Ltd, London, 1953)

Waugh, Alec, The Sugar Islands, (Cassell, London, 1958)

Williams, Eric, From Columbus to Castro: The History of the Caribbean 1492-1969, (Andre Deutsch, London, 1970)

APPENDIX

Speech delivered by V. C. Bird Snr., Prime Minister of Antigua and Barbuda at the state banquet preceding the proclamation of Independence on October 31, 1981

Your Royal Highness, Your Excellency the Governor and Lady Jacobs, Honourable Prime Ministers, Premier and Chief Ministers, Your Excellencies, Distinguished Guests, Ladies and Gentlemen.

I wish to formally express a sincere welcome to our guests who have travelled many miles, amid busy schedules, to share with us the historic occasion of our attainment of nationhood.

Your Royal Highness, it was Her Majesty the Queen who decided that you should be her representative at these celebrations. But, I am happy to declare that the people and government of Antigua and Barbuda were in full accord with Her Majesty's decision. You are, of course, no stranger here, and on previous visits you secured a permanent place in the hearts of our people by your radiance and charm.

This is, therefore, an occasion for a double celebration: Antigua and Barbuda's independence and your welcome return to our shores.

Distinguished Guests, in the midst of our elation, we feel a deep sense of humility that you have all paid us such a great honour by your presence. I need hardly tell you, my friends, that this is an emotional moment.

The road to independence has not always been smooth. Over the years by struggle and sacrifice, we achieved political advancement and then economic progress. The second task was as difficult as the first, for we inherited a one-crop economy, little infrastructure, and largely untrained and unskilled labour.

It is a tribute to the people that they took advantage of assistance from Britain, and Canada and the United States and in a few short years diversified the economy, created a successful tourist industry and produced a relatively large complement of skilled labour.

Over the last few days, as we prepared for these celebrations and looked forward to the proceedings at midnight, I could not help but reflect on the many years that led to this moment.

They were not easy years. Many brave and courageous people gave their whole lives to the cause of independence. My great regret is that some of them are not here, except in spirit, to share our joy at this time.

The movement toward independence began centuries ago when slaves resisted their captivity. Many suffered cruel ends for their presumption that freedom was their right.

But perhaps the movement really took form when the workers were galvanised to action in the 1940s. Living in houses of mud and crocus bags, unable to afford education for their children and paid a paltry wage for back breaking toil in the relentless heat of the sun, they finally rallied behind a trades union.

The union leaders could not ask for sacrifices from the people. For what more could be sacrificed by those with nothing to give? People subsisting below the poverty line could give only their lives.

Incredibly, through a remarkable reserve of human stamina, those people sacrificed even more. Sugar was king in this country at the time. Despite high profits, the plantation owners paid a pittance to the workers. Those workers could not afford even a basic diet to avoid malnutrition.

Strikes were called to pressure the owners to recognise the union and to permit it to bargain for better conditions. The workers knew that to strike would result in the loss of even small pittances which they received as wages. They knew that starvation would gnaw at their stomachs, that their children would suffer, that they would be stretched beyond human endurance.

Yet they went on strike. And they stayed on strike for six months eating wild bush and drinking hot water.

It was a formidable demonstration of a people's struggle for justice.

The workers won in the end. But it was heart breaking to see men suffer so terribly to persuade other men to be human.

And that was only one instance in a series of events where the people of this country struggled for basic rights and justice.

Tonight, the fire glows brightly, for we have, at last, arrived at the moment of independence. It is a moment to be cherished, not feared; it is a moment to rejoice, not mourn; it is a moment for hope, not despair.

My friends, we bear no ill will for the past. We know that in addition to the resolve of our people, our development, thus far, owes much to the assistance of our friends in Britain, Canada and the United States. We are gratified that we have reached this moment in a spirit of friendship and co-operation.

Our efforts now will be turned to building a free country. A country free from oppression, free from racial prejudice, free from hunger and from want.

Those efforts will not be without obstacles. But we owe it to those who planted the seeds of freedom to preserve the fruits of independence for generations yet unborn.

Tonight, it is to that task I unreservedly pledge my Government.

Thank you.

Speech delivered by V. C. Bird Snr., Prime Minister of Antigua and Barbuda at Flag Raising Ceremony on November 1, 1981

Your Royal Highness, Your Excellency the Governor-General and Lady Jacobs, Honourable Prime Ministers, Premier and Chief Minister, Your Excellencies, Distinguished Guests, Fellow Antiguans and Barbudans.

On behalf of the people of Antigua and Barbuda, I

wish to thank Her Majesty the Queen, through you, your Royal Highness, for her message of congratulations and for her expression of good wishes.

It is a message we sincerely value, for as you know, the people of this country chose to remain a Monarchy and to continue our allegiance to Her Majesty for whom we have deep affection and great respect.

We would be grateful if, in turn, you would convey to Her Majesty our best wishes and fondest regards.

I would now beg leave of Your Royal Highness to address the people of Antigua and Barbuda.

My people, this night ends three centuries of struggle for freedom. This night fulfils our unflagging hopes and satisfies our passionate desire to be free. This night marks the finest hour in our people's history. For, at last, we are charters of our own course, captains of our own ship, masters of our own destiny.

Tonight, we have severed the umbilical chord which united us with Britain. Tonight, we are an Associated State no more. Tonight, we are a nation fully formed and can take advantage of every opportunity in the world to which we have been delivered.

But, in severing the final constitutional tie with Britain, we must not act like a petulant infant. As we must be practical in all things, so we must be practical in recognising that we cannot blame today's Britain for the rule of yesterday's Empire.

Those days are gone and should be recalled only in a constructive sense: as a reminder to us never to relinquish freedom again.

It is an historical fact that we were a colony of Britain; it is a matter of record that people were exploited in this land. But equally, it is true that Britain has contributed to the development which made our Independence possible tonight.

Independence ends only our formal links with Britain. There are other more lasting links which will endure for many years to come.

As I said at the Constitutional Conference on Independence for Antigua and Barbuda last December: "This end marks a new beginning in our relations with Britain. Independence cannot erase our three centuries of association, it cannot diminish the mutual respect and regard established in the span of six generations, it can neither negate our common language nor ignore the history and tradition we share. Indeed, as two sovereign States committed to the process of democracy, to the preservation of human rights and a world free of conflict, there will be many areas in which we can co-operate in our mutual interest."

Tonight, we cast away acrimony over the past and, instead, embrace the British people as our allies and friends of the future.

My people, we are a multi-racial society. Our forefathers were Africans, English, Welsh, Scot, Portuguese and more recently, Lebanese and Syrian. Tonight, those distinctions no longer apply. Tonight, we are all re-born Antiguans and Barbudans, each with a role to play, each with a contribution to make.

Our society is based on the principle of Government of the people, by the people, for the people. That principle refers to all the people, not only to the majority of the people. As we oppose racial bigotry and prejudice in other lands, so we must eradicate any trace of it in our own society.

Always, we should demonstrate to the world our national integrity. In doing so, we must practice what we preach.

I wish now to say a special word to the youth of this Country. This Independence and the benefits, which will be its bounty, are your inheritance. You have been given what generations of your forefathers struggled and suffered to achieve.

I ask you now to cherish it. And to cherish it not only with words, but with action.

You are the future of Antigua and Barbuda and if that future is to be prosperous, if it is to be meaningful, much will depend on you. The future calls for discipline and for dedication. There is no ideal more noble, no task more rewarding, than to work for your own country's development.

The late American President, John F. Kennedy, told his people: "Think not what your country can do for you, but what you can do for your country." Tonight, I ask you to think about both. Think what your country can do for you, but think also what you must first do for your country, so that it is capable of doing for you.

My people, we are free this night. But freedom cannot exist without responsibility. The full burden of our freedom now rests squarely upon our shoulders. What we do with that freedom is our own responsibility, we can blame no other.

Part of the responsibility of freedom is to protect it. As a small developing country with little resources other than beaches, land and people, we have to safeguard our freedom by ensuring that we never become dependent again.

The ultimate safeguard of Independence is productivity. This nation, born again tonight, must commit itself to work and to work hard. For if we fail to do so, the consequence of our failure will be dependence on a new master who will, once again, dictate our policies and direct our affairs.

We must not have struggled so long and with such fortitude to exchange one master for another.

People of Antigua and Barbuda, I call on you to pledge yourselves to freedom. Rise-up to the task of protecting our Independence by creating an economically self-reliant nation, founded on the dignity of labour and the value of work.

I cannot promise that the road ahead will be smooth. I can give no assurance that if you sit idle benefits will fall in your laps like manna from heaven. But, I can promise that provided we all work together in our national interest, we will sustain our Independence with dignity and with self-respect.

Fellow Antiguans and Barbudans, we have been delivered of the Promised Land. Here we stand upon its glorious earth as it awaits only our shoulder at the wheel, our hand at the plough.

Let us go forth and be productive. Let us multiply the fruits of Independence, let us reap the rewards of labour. Let us make this a Land of glory; a land where we can say with pride: We are Antiguans and Barbudans.

Long live the nation of Antigua and Barbuda! Long live Independence!

How to get a copy of Antigua & Barbuda: A Little Bit of Paradise

To order your copy simply write direct to Hansib Publishing (address below) including payment of £25.00 plus a charge for postage & packing @ £3.50 per book UK and £7.00 overseas (surface mail). Please allow 28 days for delivery.

Other titles available from Readers Book Club

DOMINICA: NATURE ISLAND OF THE CARIBBEAN
320 pages, richly illustrated in full colour, capturing the hitherto little known beauty of this Caribbean country and offers a brief account of its sometimes turbulent history and rich culture. Practical information for the visitor is also included. **£19.95** plus p&p @ £3.50 UK and £7.00 overseas (surface mail) per book.

INDIA IN THE CARIBBEAN
Edited by Dr David Dabydeen and Dr Brinsley Samaroo
A collection of essays, poems and prose by leading Indo-Caribbean scholars and writers, on East Indian history and culture in the Caribbean. **£8.95**.

100 GREAT WESTINDIAN TEST CRICKETERS
from Challenor to Richards by Bridgette Lawrence with Reg Scarlett
Through the eyes of the leading players of the last 60 years, the rise of Westindian Test Cricket is traced from its beginnings at Lord's in 1928.
£14.95 plus p&p @ £3.50 UK and £7.00 overseas (surface mail) per book.

BENEVOLENT NEUTRALITY: INDIAN GOVERNMENT POLICY AND LABOUR MIGRATION TO BRITISH GUIANA 1854-1884
By Dr Basdeo Mangru
A detailed, scholarly essay on Indian migration, which, for the first time, studies the Indian background of the indentured labourers and explains the economic, political and cultural factors which encouraged migration. **£12.95**.

KING OF THE CARNIVAL AND OTHER STORIES
By Willi Chen
A unique collection of short stories from the Caribbean, capturing the violence, trickery, pathos and racial comedy of the Trinidadian society. Chen writes in a great sweep of energy and from a deeply humane perspective, investing his characters with the capacity for laughter, suffering and redemption. **£5.95**.

RASTA AND RESISTANCE From Marcus Garvey to Walter Rodney
By Dr Horace Campbell
A study of the Rastafarian Movement in all its manifestations, from the streets of Birmingham, England to the Shashamane Settlement in Ethiopia. **£8.95**.

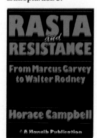

SPEECHES BY ERROL BARROW
Edited by Yussuf Haniff
The late Errol Barrow, former Prime Minister of Barbados, was among the dominant figures in the political life of his country for more than two decades. This collection represents a portion of some of his significant speeches, reflecting the kind of philosophy and thinking that guided his actions both in and out of government. **£10.95**.

INSEPERABLE HUMANITY An Anthology of Reflections of Shridath Ramphal.
Introduced and edited by Ron Sanders
Former Commonwealth Secretary-General, Shridath Ramphal was, for more than a decade, in the front rank of spokespersons on international issues. This collection addresses his remarkable contribution to the causes of decolonisation, Third World development and world peace. **£14.95**.

THE GREAT MARCUS GARVEY
By Liz Mackie
A lively, informed and readable account of the work of one of the greatest black leaders in this century. Despite harassment and eventual imprisonment, Garvey, now honoured as a Jamaican National hero, was able to instil a sense of pride, discipline and resolve in his followers, campaigning against the injustices of colonial rule. **£4.95**.

A NEW SYSTEM OF SLAVERY: THE EXPORT OF INDIAN LABOUR OVERSEAS 1830-1920
By Professor Hugh Tinker
When first published, this book was the first comprehensive survey of a hitherto neglected and only partially known migration - the export of Indians to supply labour for worldwide plantation cash-crop production. **£11.99**.

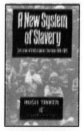

HANSIB

To order any of the above titles please write; enclosing Cheques/POs/Money Orders plus p&p at £1.50 (UK) and £3.00 (overseas surface mail) per book (unless otherwise stated), made payable to Readers Book Club; to: Readers Book Club, Third Floor, Tower House, 141-149 Fonthill Road, London N4 3HF. Tel: (44) (0)171 281 1191, Fax (44) (0)171 263 9656.
Please allow 28 days for delivery.

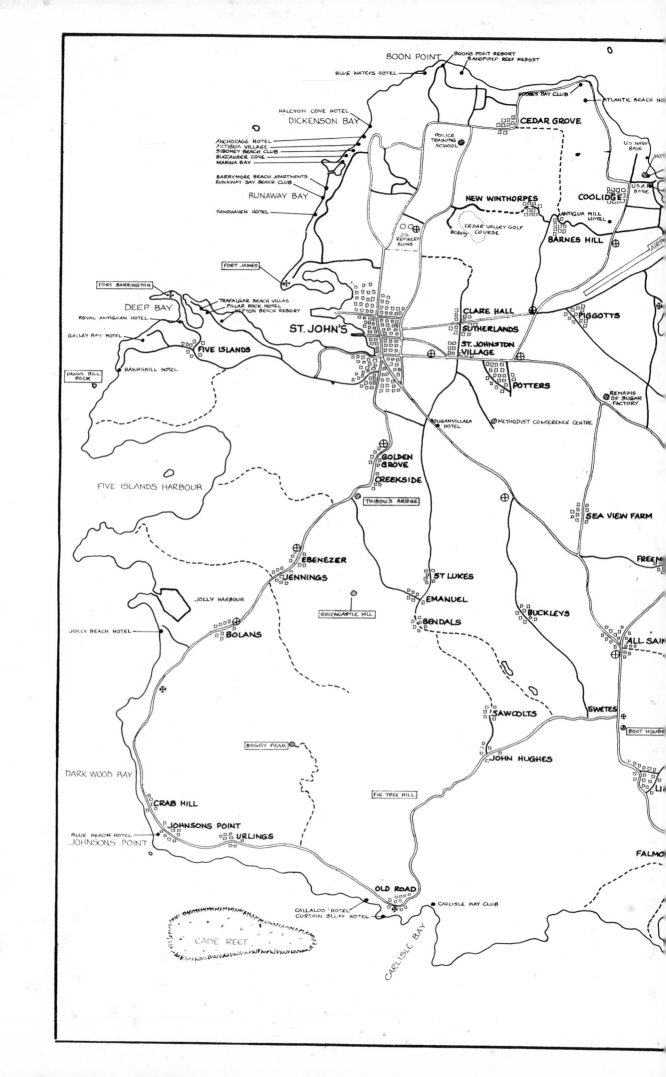